Fowler's
SNARE

Assassination and Resurrection
of the Human Spirit

ABBY FLANDERS

ISBN
978-1-954168-93-0 (Paperback)
978-1-954168-92-3 (eBook)

*This book is dedicated to the
Power of the Lord in all His
majesty, and to Nellie Geraldine
Boyd Flanders and James
Flanders, Sr., my beloved parents
whose sacrifice and support
give me reasons to thrive.*

Table of Contents

Prologue

There are many people who find themselves caught in "survival mode," learning "the game" and how to play it well. This often means deception, manipulation, presenting oneself in a way others might trust actions taken, words spoken, and professionalism expected. The victimization comes as a double-edged sword. Generally, the person who is demonstrating the self-absorbed behavior has been told, or experienced what happens in lean times when money and mercy are both depleting rapidly, and there is no escape from the proverbial season of discontent.

This is dedicated to those who are on both ends of a dilemma that has become an epidemic, and like a disease, it is causing a spiritual manifestation of cankers and sores on the face of humanity. The victimizers are also the victims of an outrageous plot conceived by dark forcesto kill, steal, and destroy. Both sides are in the throes of a delusion that begins in the mind with the thought that we "simple specimen of flesh" have control over the destinies of ourselves and others. This thought speaks to our narcissistic inner being, secretly whispering commands that suppress the potential in others as well as ourselves. It all hinders on the mindset that regales the importance of collecting things and crucifying human beings in an effort to feel above the fringes of our fragile lives; lives that can be taken instantaneously and eternally without even the mist of remembrance. Even those who believe they have gained in wealth and power are destined to lose. Only their legacy remains intact, and that is always subject to interpretation and scrutiny.

There is one thing that unites the separation between the rich and the poor, the employer and the employee, the young and the old, and that is the fact that our flesh is terminal. It is only what we condition our minds to censor, our beliefs to accept, and our hearts to feel our last moments on this earth.

A dark forest can lead to an enlightened field of sobriety. It is the blinding passageway that fills the heart with both brittle thorns and somber sympathies. Finding the balance between the two can be fraught with disillusionment and disguise. Often what guides the traveler is spiritual instinct, yet the path can be strewn with denigrating obstacles unwittingly placed on the trail by the pathfinder. Losing the way is tantamount to finding the purpose. This constant war between the fowler and his prey can lead to the ultimate light of salvation. The snares in which we appear to be caught are releasing our spirits into the arms of the most powerful and beloved pioneer in the universe.

It is this Force that conquers the midnights that rise in front of each of us as we travel this road, flying through the dust storms of outrageous fortunes and misfortunes. Suddenly, we are trapped by an event that is so demeaning and tortuous that even a prayer cannot relegate the spirit to a peaceful escape.

When I began this journey of writing about the spiritual assassinations of friends, along with my own life path from darkness to dawn, my beloved mother had just made her transition to the life beyond. I was caring for my father, who had recently become immobile, and in need of assistance for his basic human needs. A quiet house once livened only by parental voices of morning greetings and sweet expressions of endearment had become a center of caregiver traffic with raising volumes dictating patient needs, and often their personal meal preferences. Most of them were dedicated professionals who had come to love my parents and instinctively know their desires and needs intuitively. Others nodded off during the most crucial care periods and required some nudging and reprimands during their shifts. I did not believe I could ever survive the death of my parents, regardless of the natural life cycle, age, or realistic understanding that, as Stevie Wonder's Visions song prognosticated, "All things have an ending." Ecclesiastes makes it more succinct. "To everything there is a season, and a time to every purpose under the heaven: a time to be born, and a time to die; a time to plant, and a time to pluck up that which is planted, A time to kill, and a time to heal; a time to break down, and a time to build up; A time to weep, and a time to laugh...." Ecclesiastes 3:1-4. This would become my long season of weeping; a season that challenges faith and encourages the enemy's propensity to admonish and disillusion Christians and their beliefs. When my father passed unexpectedly, I dissected my life from the seed in which he and my mother planted, ultimately delivering the fruit of me, my purpose for living, and the depth of my soul's integrity. Even though I was always the cheerleader encouraging others, it was virtually impossible to elevate my heart, mind, soul, and spirit. My father died eight months and one day after my mother's transition. The day after my mother died, my aunt passed away. Four months after my father died, my uncle made his transcendence into heaven. Before death gave birth to my descending spirit, I was experiencing some major health issues. My best friend Judy Meredith, and my most generous, kind and loving friends, Freda Barker and Dave Fiske travelled with me to Baltimore's Johns Hopkins Hospital for some comprehensive tests that determined I had a dangerous condition that needed to be watched diligently throughout my life. These three people became my rock: resurrecting the core of my being and guiding me into the next life scene. Later, when my heart required repair, it was my friends Caryle Bennett, Billy Malone, Mable Rhodim, and Gail Walker who walked the path of healing with me, plus my Judy Meredith and my amazing Aunt Dianne. Fortunately, I have never really become apprehensive about my own life cycle, or the obstacles that test my health; however, it is always good to know there are human angels in the wings of your devastation who can take the reins when something puts you in a catatonic state of spiritual regression.

I found some solace in writing this book. Reminiscing about the pain suffered by friends and acquaintances that spurred thoughts about how we are able, because of the Holy Spirit, to sustain the horror of human tragedy, and step into the next scene in the script of our lives. Acclimating to losses even while we incessantly grip our hearts from the pain of loss is the beginning of the spiritual resurrection that comes from faith. When other catastrophic events follow, it can be a hell storm that requires prolific prayer, perpetual bible reading, and proficient partnerships with fellow comrades in Christ. Less than a year after my father's death, which was May 25, 2012, a new, and more distinctive enemy attack evolved from the hedges of complacency. My mammograms had been infrequent, and there were other medical exams that were appropriate for a woman of my chronological years that should have been conducted. One day when my stomach was pierced by a razor-sharp pain, I went to another doctor who insisted that I get all the missing tests required, including a mammogram. I was exceptionally nonchalant when the technician pressed my breast against a cold hard surface. Requesting that I hold my breath, she took x-rays. I joked a bit about holding my breath to the point of passing out. (Smoking shortens your breath at first and your life ultimately). She hinted in a subtle way that I would probably be called in for a second test. I thanked her and joyfully walked out of the room, my mind fixated on church work, the night's big blockbuster and intriguing television shows. I did take the test again, only this time a doctor discussed the pattern of cells that were viewed from his microscopic medical analysis. He indicated that this exam was probably telling the story of a malignancy. The next test would be a biopsy. Once again, I discarded any thoughts of cancer because it was something I could not process. Basically, I felt good, so there was no reason to fear. After all, I had already been "pre-disastered" to borrow a phrase from the movie "The World According to Garp." In the movie, it was after a plane crashed into Garp's new home that he uttered the phrase in order to assure his new bride that nothing else could go wrong. Just as in the movie, things can continue to go wrong for a time that seems to be an eternity in our natural minds. I came back to get the results and was told that I had breast cancer.

Breast cancer is a game changer for those who experience it. Breast cancer puts in perspective the frailty of life on earth, and the possibility of the impossible if the spirit is lifted to heavenly realms. My journey with the disease has been hopefully short lived. There was no chemo, no radiation, and no medication; however, this medical journey morphed into a profound psychological destiny. Many patients wade through the murky waters of dark deception and plummeting emotional discord. Even the strongest of the faithful feel their mortality shifting into a climax. Death becomes a definable reality that must be faced even in the throes of celestial petitions for time enough to create something that could leave a positive legacy. There was no husband or children who would miss me or request a reprieve from the physical agony that often follows a cancer diagnosis. As far as I could tell, my life was a series of scenes from an unnatural disaster that could be mocked in the shadows of pernicious chatter. Somehow, I imagined my parents on the other side of this drama with their hands beckoning me to the freedom that could be claimed beyond the agony of my existence. My spirit had been assassinated by the erroneous thoughts that plague the soul and dim the spirit when the fowler extends his snare in pursuit of another victim. Life can be a series of setting suns, with souls wading in pools of darkness fanning the flames of their last ember of light. It is at this hour, this shade of midnight when an epiphany drapes the mind of the weary wanderer. You pain is your purpose. Since we all carry a purpose for being here, a light that is planted inside us for the role that we play in this dramedy called life, we must reside in some darkness. Light cannot shine in light. It can only shine in darkness as a part of a collective illumination for the salvation of humanity. Although many scenes in our scripts leave us weeping, if the mind and the spirit can alter the effects of our theatrical experiences, there may even be a few laughs in the face of the adversity. The fowler detests such reactions because his goal is to annihilate all hopes and decimate all dreams that sustain any spiritual awakening.

When I began writing this book, I believed I had entered and exited my most damaging tornado, only to find there was a terrifying typhoon lurking beneath the surface in the near distance; undetected and unmeasured, and only seen by celestial vision.

It is the fowler who, through his studies of character, ego, and heart, can mix the ingredients for dark passageways each traveler's journey can be diminished. Although the journey begins with God, it is often interrupted by the plots, plans, and schemes of the Master of Malfeasance, the ruler of the corruptible abyss filled with inhumane horror. We only rise from the pit of the beast when we diligently seek the light from which we began; the one that flutters in ebony tides yet guides the "sin sick soul." The stories in this book are real, but the names have all been changed to protect the innocent and shield the identities of the not so innocent.

"Surely He will save you from the fowler's snare and the deadly pestilence." (Psalm 91:3)

Forward

My husband often says, "Life is a process." Indeed, it is, for in our journey's lifecycle, no matter how we try to avoid them, we have brushes with our deepest fears - serious illness, the loss of a child, a crippling car crash, financial despair, and the cruel and demonic behavior of others who, like wicked puppeteers, pull and tug at our spiritual lifeline, trying to cast us into their fiery snares of hell. It is all we can do to survive the experiences, to keep our composure, to not panic and to continue to believe in the power source that is the one true healer; our constant companion, and yes, our slayer of leviathans who appear before us in sheep's clothing, but who ultimately strip away their pretentious layers to reveal their ungodly intent to crush us.

Abigail Flanders, a prolific writer and orator, and my dear friend, has eloquently expressed, through her writing of THE FOWLER'S SNARE: THE ASSASSINATION AND RESURRECTION OF THE HUMAN SPIRIT, her own reflections of life and its processes. She brilliantly weaves the dark threads of life's challenges into the bright primary shades of hope, faith and steadfastness needed to overcome struggles. We have either experienced similar feats during life's process or we know someone who has managed countless escapes from the fowler's snare. We know that, because we are still here.

Ms. Flanders understands the struggles we all face regardless of our station in life. While reading this book, I was reminded of my own melees and more importantly, how they were invariably resolved. This book forced me to reminisce times gone by, to relive the fowler's snares in my

own life, and to ponder the escapes from each entrapment. There have been numerous occasions during life's process where I decided to not only survive, but also, with our Higher Being's guidance, to conquer the enemy, ultimately witnessing his self-destruction in his own snare.

An adoptee, my mother passed away when I was only 19. I was a sophomore in college. Oh, how devastating it was to lose my best friend. The thoughts and worries bolted, ravaging through the crevices of my brain with lightning streak quickness. I was an only child. What am I to do now? How can I live without my mother? How could I go back to college? Who could I turn to for that motherly support? In the moment of emotional turmoil, I chose to continue to pursue my college degree, though that chapter did not end there. Shortly after my mother's death, my father was found in our home, lying in a pool of blood. He had been shot in the head. Once again, I was faced with a decision of whether to complete my college degree or resolve to work in Gary Indiana's steel mills. I could have made a decent but hard-earned living. Ultimately, I finished college, and not surprisingly, much of the steel business folded over the next few years leaving scores of people out of work. I have found that THE FOWLER'S SNARE is an excellent resource to help the reader to place life's journey into perspective. If we can occasionally reflect on our own experiences by vicariously living the stories of others, then we are reminded that life is a process and that we can make it through and escape the fowler's snare.

-Dr. Judy Alsobrooks Meredith-
(wife of Human Rights Leader, James Meredith)

A Candle in the Night

A ray of sun, a glimpse of light
A constant prayer to end the night
A candle burns day by day
Revealing God's favor as we pray

*"Heal the sick, raise the dead, and cleanse those
who have leprosy, drive out demons."*

(Matthew 10:8)

CHAPTER ONE

"Chaos, COVID & Confusion"

Some people walk quietly into the light, understanding their purpose and life mission. Others struggle with the shadows of existence, braving the elements of whimsical Fate and the fog of erroneous choices. This has been my walk, my struggle through the endless corridors of relentless Fate, grabbing on the doorways of a spirituality that probably saved my life. The corridors of life can sometimes be littered with strange dark figures, distorted by the undeniable midnight inside a jaundice eye. Viewing the world through rose-colored glasses can shade circumstances in a way that shatters hope. When the glasses are removed, sometimes hope, happiness, and any semblance of what is and is not good in the world can be distorted.

2013, the annual mammogram was due, so like many other women, I climbed into my grayish Toyota. Singing a Motown hit from the seventies, I drove to the area hospital laboratory. The cold steel gadget that presses far too hard against a tender breast caused some slight pain, but mostly I was concerned with getting home in time to see Judge Mathis and have a simple meal, courtesy of any fast-food place with a fish menu. "Hold your breath..." the technician said in a soft, but authoritarian voice. It seemed like hours before she told me to breathe. One time, she never said "breathe" and I finally had to ask her permission to take a much-needed breath. 'I thought you were trying to kill me,' I said chuckling. So, did she. After the exam, she looked at me with serious extended pupils and said, "I think you may have to come back here for a biopsy." I ignored her ghostly look and ghastly tone, began dressing, and said "Alright." Taking notice of my cavalier demeanor, she reiterated her statement in a louder tone with emphasis on the word "biopsy." I thought, 'Is she trying to alarm me? I know I am fine. There are no lumps in my breasts.' "Fine," I said while reaching for some hurry, as my grandfather often mused, to get out of there. It was only a few days later when the phone rang, and she called me to tell me she was ready to schedule the biopsy.

When I arrived in the cold, sterile, Examining Room, the physician came in to introduce himself. He was an affable man in the proverbial pristine white lab coat. "So, are you nervous?" He asked in the traditional 'I am here for you if you want to cry' voice. Unphased by the melodrama, I said, "No, I'm not." "Good...Good, Miss Flanders. I am going to position you, then make sure I have everything I need for the biopsy. I'll be right back." I was turned upside down on the examining table with my breasts dangling down lifelessly through metallic holes on each side. I waited in this position, exposing my loose breasts to the floor while listening to the doctor make small talk about his golf game to another doctor outside the door. After about twenty minutes, the nurse said, "Where is Dr. X? I think I hear him outside the door, but I wonder how long he's going to be out there?"

My patience had worn out as much as the gravity from my position on the table. "He's out there talking about golf," I said angrily. "Tell him he can do that later. I need him to take this biopsy and let me go home." The nurse quickly escaped to the hallway, and the doctor came in behind her. "I understand you were complaining about me talking about my golf game. Are you alright? I sighed heavily. 'Yes, I did complain about you being outside for so long. I am half naked with my breasts hanging to the ground. You can discuss your golf game AFTER you do this biopsy.' I said with a small nervous laugh. I wondered how many nervous women had been in the same position, hanging upside down on a table, breasts nearly touching the floor and waiting endlessly for some narcissistic doctor to complete his happy talk before plowing inside their chest; the protrusion that once adorned beautiful blouses and low-cut dresses, mining for a malignancy that could erase their confidence and blur the lines between life and death. How many ladies wrestled with how they would break the news to their spouses and children if the test burst their desires to exit this planet with everything, they brought into it, including both breasts? Time can be a dear friend, or a ruthless enemy when you are awaiting a call that can permanently change your life. Tick...Tock...the synchronic sounds of a time piece in a quiet room can deafen the music in a faithful heart. The interruption of a phone ring can jolt you like the bruising cacophony of firecrackers and stick bombs tossed carelessly in the night. You are commanded to appear at the hospital for the verdict. Then, there is the cancer verdict. Guilty as charged. After you discover you have cancer every breath in the room ceases, especially yours. The first ten seconds after hearing the words "I'm sorry. You have cancer," I ceased to exist. It appeared to be a strange dream I was having, and I wanted to wake up quickly. The next ten seconds, I thought, 'I wonder how God is going to use this.' I learned a long time ago God does not bring anything into your life without using it for a higher purpose. I never asked, 'Why me?' Realizing how many have succumb to breast cancer, I understood the moments in life that I had taken for granted; jumping rope as a child, dancing to Motown hits as a teenager, and laughing so hard that my body went limp with delight as an aging adult. God had been good to me and I had always been blessed.

A nurse slumped in a corner turning shades of red was the first thing I noticed when I came out of surgery. My left breast had been removed, the mastectomy was a medical success, but the nurse's face revealed something more telling. "Your heartbeat plummeted, and we had to call a crash cart," she said as I released the clouds of anesthesia from my eyes to focus on her image. I was nonchalant about her words. I thought, 'Yeah, but I am still here.'

Five years later, I was scheduled for a colonoscopy, a regular examination, hopefully without drama. My eyes remained closed, yet during the anesthetized sleep, eyes closed shut, I saw an orange ball emerge inside the room. It came closer and grew larger with every inch it traveled. When it approached me at its closest point, it vanished, and I opened my eyes in amazement. There was a screeching sound during the transition. I heard the mumblings of the young nurses around me commenting on me as if I had lost my life. Slowly, I opened my eyes to see the grimace on the doctor's face as he stared at me. "Do you have a cardiologist?" He asked with the look doctors give when they are about to give you bad news. 'Not really. I see someone once every two years or so.' "What's your cardiologist's name? I am calling whoever it is now. You can either see a cardiologist, or go to the Emergency Room, but whatever you do, you cannot go home." I gathered it was another serious moment in my life. I slowly got up off the gurney, went to the dressing room and contemplated the serious tone in the colon doctor's voice. As I walked to the lobby, the doctor came in to tell me, "I have called your doctor's office. He is not available, but I made a 1:30pm appointment for you today. It was already 11:30, so I called a friend who had an Uber waiting to take me from my house to the waiting cardiologist.

The cardiologist's examination indicated that my heart valve required replacement. I would undergo open heart surgery to replace the failing valve with that of a cow or a pig. Personally, I was routing for the cow. 'After a certain age, pork can be detrimental to your health,' I concluded as I searched for the humor in the situation. Understandably, I was apprehensive about the surgery. The average stay for a procedure such as mine was a week. I was in Intensive Care for sixteen days before being transferred to a regular hospital room. Then, there was an additional nine day stay in a Rehabilitation Center. I kept repeating a line from the Andy Griffin Show, "Just a fun time all the way around."

Illness is like living on a desert without sunlight, a cold desolate dry place with wet sand seeping through your limp body. You can see others across a river of laughter and euphoria, but they can neither see you nor touch you. It is a lonely shadow of urgency in a forest filled with brown leaves and broken limbs. Surviving the experience of illness requires constant communication with a Holy negotiator while making your case inside a celestial court of empathy and mercy.

The heart surgery released a fatigue in me that projected depression once unknown and twice as frustrating. Trying to manipulate steps, or simply walk to the bathroom was more than a chore. It was an adventure like climbing a towering snow crest mountain in your bare feet. It can be inexplicably numbing, draining your faith bank and minimalizing your push towards existence. Time and prayer are restorative measures for realigning your position with God and once again surviving the experience. However, just as you begin adjusting to one obstacle, another drifts carelessly in your life path.

My heart surgery occurred in 2019, which I marked as a very toxic year. Surely 2020 would yield the harvest of rose petals from the thorns. Although it was difficult to elevate my spirits above the divisive turmoil of the times, my faith had been exercised by the various health scares of previous years. My waiting soul pined for the glory of God to trample the unrighteous and vigorously take up the cause against the blight of inhumanity. Suddenly, there was a new nemesis called COVID; an indiscriminate virus that was whimsically attacking the vulnerable. It was leaving a path of death and destruction in its wake, and no one was immune to its demonic preeminence; least of all me.

Someone with whom I had proximity tested positive for the COVID virus. I heard this information second hand and rushed to make an appointment for a test. I casually perused messages on my cell phone. There was no apprehension about the test. Surely with every other sickness I endured and my careful quarantine methods, I was certain I would be negative. No such luck! The Health Department notice on my phone read "You have tested positive for the COVID virus. We will call you soon to advise you." Honestly, I was incredulous. 'There's no way I have COVID,' I thought. As my best friend, Judy's daughter exclaimed breaking a verb for emphasis, "Do she have to have EVERYTHING?" It was my question as well. I was closely following the chaos in our country and bemoaning the ridiculous deaths of Black youth who continued to be the target of unmitigated violence and injustice. This kind of malaise can shake a spirit and leave a nation diminished and stained. "What the world needs now is love sweet love," kept rolling around in my head. This national crisis and the fiery fuel of loquacious bigotry create dis-ease within itself. Add to that the unknown symptoms and consequential nature of this unpredictable virus and there is a new element of despair.

Reflecting on my youth, I can recall being a young girl with pig tails flopping in the wind while elderly cantors in a cacophony of voices sang, "When you walk through a storm, hold your head up high, and don't be afraid of the dark…Walk on through the wind, walk on through the rain, and you'll never walk alone…" The wind of change in age, body, and above health was blowing a cold chill through my defiant body. I could feel a shaking from my feet to my head, like a volcano erupting leaving the lava of chills and fever throughout its path. Cold soaking sweat penetrated my gown, drenching its way from hem to neckline. Three times, I forced my lethargic filled body to change my wet night clothes and replace them temporarily with another clean pre-saturated gown. My stomach ached with nausea, and the small morsels that were digested came up in roar of rejection for three consecutive days. Through it all, I learned to trust that all would be well with me. I was not in a hospital, and I survived the malicious mayhem of infection that manically destroyed hundreds of thousands, many of whom prayed harder than I. Their prayers were not weaker, nor did they go unanswered. God welcomed them home because their work here was finished. They had done what God put them here to do, including becoming the martyrs who served as examples of quiet heroism in the face of abject infirmity. Some were people dear to my heart, others were parents, grandparents, sisters, brothers, daughters, and sons. All stricken by an invisible enemy who entered and exited their lives without regard to their color, creed, nationality, religion, or sexual preference. COVID is an equal opportunity destroyer that continues to permeate the nation as of this writing. This should bring many to their knees, side by side without color, nationality, religious, or sexual preferences. The preference here should be the healing of our country, and the world. It is only through this mutual energy of collective human conscience that we can exist separately or together.

The Healing Hand of God

Fret not my soul in great despair
The Lord protects every strand of hair
And with His love we rest in peace
His faithful healing, He will release

"He will command his angels concerning you,
and they will lift you up in their hands, so that you
will not strike your foot against a stone."

Matthew 4:5

CHAPTER TWO

"Nellie and the Novena"

If you live long enough, you will hear many stories about the wonders of what many consider unnatural or paranormal events. Spiritually speaking, they are called miracles, and they are totally natural to most believers. The concept of an invisible Superior Being of whom you can call upon in the hours of desperation is the basis of religious precepts. Contemporary parables abound with individual dilemmas that culminate in things beyond the contemplation of the human mind. Yet, those who understand biblical doctrine are led by the premise that the Great Shepherd never "leaves or forsakes" His flock.

The real test of religious or spiritual beliefs comes when there is sickness, death, depression, and frustration with the inevitable problems of this unpredictable world. We control nothing in our existence and any attempts at planning ahead are fruitless. There is an adage, "if you want to make God laugh, make plans." Prayer and supplication are the vehicles for obtaining and sustaining a life fraught with pain-filled emotional turmoil. It is through our faith that we believe in things we cannot see and see the things many cannot believe.

Nellie Flanders grew up in a faith-filled loving home in a southern state where manners and dignity are as precious as diamonds and rubies. The youngest and only girl in a sea of male siblings, she lived the doctrine of spiritual compliance, as did her five brothers. It was a time of benign liaisons when hand holding was tantamount to lip locking, and the expectations of a suitor were a soda and a smile. The 1940's was an era of platitudes and mundane activities that expressed an innocent joy for those connected by the fate of their time. World War II had come to an end, and young people throughout the nation were marrying hurriedly and families were growing rapidly. Nellie married musician and World War II veteran, James Flanders when they were both just out of their teens. They grew up together with childhood memories of nursery rhyming songs, and frolicking friendships that would last a lifetime. Their first child would turn out to be a double blessing, identical twins that mirrored the image of their doting father. Life consisted of schoolwork, mostly for Nellie who was attending the local university in pursuit of a degree in education. Her husband, James had already received a degree in the social sciences; however, he was a musical prodigy; racing through childhood playing both piano and saxophone with friends who would later find world acclaim for their musical prowess. James decided on a different course of action due to a solid sense of family obligation. Traveling at a moment's performing at jazz concerts would be irresponsible in his mind.

The winters seemed colder in the 40's even in the south, and fur coats were as plentiful there as they were in the northern states. Breezes cut through the skin like piercing blades that scarred the bone, leaving painful prickly sparks in their wake. Coughing and sneezing were commonplace, and most ladies carried their hankies not only to cover their mouths, but to demonstrate their daintiness and cultural upbringing. Nellie found herself on the other end of a coughing spell that seemed to last for weeks. She determined that the frost in the air was wreaking havoc on her small frame and a heavier coat must be the remedy. Adding to her malaise was the constant chasing of two rambunctious precocious girls who kept her constantly on her feet, running from room to room. As the coughing became more relentless, Nellie, with the insistence of James, decided to seek medical relief. She went to the family physician who gave her tests to determine the origin of her cough, recognizing it was more than a simple cold when blood spewed from the saliva flowing from her mouth. The result was devastating. Nellie had tuberculosis, a disease that was considered fatal at the time.

Tuberculosis is a highly communicable infectious disease that produces nodules in the body, primarily in the lungs. There was no known cure during the 1940's, and it was also a social stigma because of the mystery of its origin. Like many other diseases, tuberculosis was misunderstood; therefore, it became the fodder for rumor mills connecting the cause with poverty, uncleanness, malnutrition, and overcrowded conditions. Medical research had not reached a point of discovery for cause, cure, or adequate treatment of tuberculosis during this era. Later, it was discovered that anyone could become infected by carriers with a cough, and even through unpasteurized milk. This discovery prompted legislation that required a mandatory pasteurization of milk. During the 1940's post-war era, there was an epidemic of tuberculosis because symptoms were often hidden from its carriers until the disease developed into contagion. It was known to lie dormant in many of its victims, so many people were unaware that they were carriers or threatened with illness, and more often, death. Writers D.H. Lawrence in 1930 and George Orwell in 1950 died from tuberculosis, along with the internationally acclaimed star of "Gone with the Wind," Vivien Leigh in 1967.

Sanatoriums in scenic, yet distant places, generally in wooded areas far away from populated cities were used as quarantine for those stricken with the disease. The length of stay in such institutions ranged from fourteen to twenty-six months. It was here that Nellie was sent right after her diagnosis. Her condition appeared to worsen as she lay helplessly in bed unable to move or turn her body. The excruciating pain in her chest, and the discomfort from lying on her side often brought draping tears to her eyes. The thought of death permeated her mind as she prayed for her small children and her husband, then wondered what would happen to them if she would succumb to this incurable illness. Doctors were less than optimistic, but they plied her with antibiotics hoping for the best. It was not working, and she felt the steely sting of impending doom when nurses turned her from side to side every two hours.

Weeks shifted into months, and then years, as she found herself trapped in a reclining position with the bed and disease as her prisoners. Although she welcomed the sight of her beloved twins, her husband, her brothers, and her friends during their brief and cautious visits, they were a reminder of a life now vacant, and a spirit depleted of hope and happiness. She prayed continuously expecting a miracle but found her faith languishing in a pool of sweat from layers of blankets that appeared ubiquitously across her hospital bed.

Janet was a childhood friend with whom Nellie traipsed in her state of growth through wooded terrain, often leaving miniature footprints in the soft dirt. Although they were both now in their mid-twenties, Janet considered Nellie to be the sister she never had; and since Nellie never had a sister, she welcomed the newly elected kinship. Visiting Nellie in a place nearly a hundred miles from their home, in what Janet considered to be a desolate forbidding environment, was extremely difficult. She remembered how both she and Nellie were consumed with sorrow ten years earlier when she lost her father. Then there was the pounding loneliness of losing her mother nearly six years before tuberculosis overpowered her world.

Janet was a devout catholic who attended daily mass, said her rosary at night, and read her bible as often as possible. She prayed for Nellie and tried to uplift her spirits by reading passages from the Old and New Testament, encouraging Nellie to repeat them so she could put them to memory. Janet also asked the church for assistance in helping Nellie's recovery in her body and with her faith walk. She realized the difficulty of walking through a long tumultuous storm of illness even for someone like Nellie who believed and trusted in the Lord. Janet's priest told her to do a novena, a nine-day prayer in which a candle is lit each day. The priest recalled stories of astonishing results for the recipients of novenas.

It was a winter day, bitterly cold in the mountainous region that housed the sanatorium. An unusual gust of wind and snowfall combed the area making it resemble a Christmas card rather than a hospital. The sole of Janet's boots was covered with traces of white when she entered Nellie's room. Nellie glared at her shoes in wonderment. It had been a long time since she had seen any part of nature, particularly snow. Janet walked over to her bed and softly rubbed her head with holy water from her church. "Nellie, I have decided to say a novena for you," she said in an almost sacredly soft voice. "What is a novena?" Nellie asked weakly. "It is a nine-day prayer that we practice in the Catholic religion. Every day I will pray for you and light a candle. On the ninth day, you will sit up, get up, walk, and be well." Nellie gazed at her admiring her sincerity and managing a heartfelt smile. "You'll see, Nellie. Nine days from now, you will be so well that they'll kick you out of this place and tell you not to come back!"

The first night of the prayer, Nellie wept silently, praying for the miracle that was promised by her childhood friend. She asked God to give her this gift, and in return she would tell the story of this miracle as her testimony throughout the remainder of her life. The second night, she discovered that she could slightly move herself in the bed, a feat which had eluded her for nearly two years. Although it was a seemingly minor victory to be able to adjust her right arm, she recognized the change and immediately associated it with the novena. The third night, the nurse admired the effort Nellie appeared to be putting into her recovery. There was a lilt in her voice even laughter on her tongue, and a renewed hope that she would soon see her husband and children in their home instead of from a reclining position in a hospital room. Every day brought new capabilities that were once taken for granted, but now celebrated as gigantic feats. Finally, on the ninth day, she sat up for the first time in two years without a nurse's arm or the elevation of a pillow. The doctor was amazed and intrigued by her rapid progress, particularly when Nellie requested that she walk to the bathroom leaning on her nurse's arm. Initially, her legs were wobbly from the stiffness of immobility, but she was convinced she would be able to make it through the darkened doorway of her destination. Slowly, but steadily her feet touched the ground for the first time, each step more assured than the last. When she reached the bathroom, she was jubilant, celebrating her victory like an Olympic champion who just received a gold medal. It was at that moment, a shadow passed from the room taking human form with roaring laughter echoing through the room and down the hallway. Her faithful friend made the trek to the wood congested hospital to examine the results of her prayer vigil. Janet jumped into the bathroom, nearly knocking down the dutiful nurse who was holding Nellie's arm. "I told you God would bring you through. Do you remember? This is the ninth day! Praise the Lord." Nellie broke into tears gurgling thank you's to God. Two weeks later, after showing remarkable recovery from what was presumed to be a fatal disease, Nellie Flanders left the sanatorium and returned to her home with a caution from her physician that she should not have children for at least five years. Her story was written in a journal of medicine, sans her identity. Two years later, on March 24, 1951, she defied the odds and had a daughter, a best friend, and confidante, Abigail Loretta Flanders. The following year, she birthed her only son, James Flanders, Jr.

Nellie Geraldine Boyd Flanders was my mother, who went home to be with Jesus on September 24, 2011. I stayed with her during her last night on earth and watched as her spirit left her body to be reunited with her departed family members and friends, including Janet, but most of all her loving Savior who carried her through the storms of life. The years after her bought with TB were filled with generosity, caring and concern for the sick. Even during her illnesses, she made phone calls to ailing and shut-in church members, sent fruit to her neighbors, and inspired hundreds of children as an elementary school teacher and mentor. She was my best friend and the person I loved best in this spiritually divided universe.

There was a spiritual division within Nellie Flanders, a war against faith from the omnipresent dark destroyer. Doctors, uncertain of things beyond their scientific knowledge, continuously chanted, like a mantra, her deathly fate. It was analogous to a separation from the promise of an omnipresent God and the denigration of a body wrenched in anguish. Her prayers, those of her family, and spiritually enlightened friends sustained her; however, the wounding of her spirit was palpable. Jesus arose on the third day after His crucifixion, as promised. Is it that difficult to believe that He can raise a sick mother, wife, and follower from her bed of affliction in nine days? Nellie Flanders lived her remaining sixty-two years giving this, and other testimonies regarding the empowerment that develops by trusting in the Lord. She had other spiritual storms, too many to recount in these pages, but through it all, her faith never wavered, and her trust never faltered. Through it all, the fowler failed.

Invisible Warriors

I am what I am despite my fate
Beloved for my climb, now the source of debate
Being my who through loss and gain
Releases my soul and buries my pain.

*"Fear not, for I have redeemed you; I have
called you by name, you are mine."*

(Isaiah 43:2)

CHAPTER THREE

Invisible Warriors

Invisible. Discarded. Ignored. Great weapons of mass destruction do not always come in metallic form. Consider how it feels to be treated as if you do not exist or banished from someone's life as if you were dead. The enemy uses his best torture methods to secure a negative reaction in his victims. Some of the best examples of this type of spiritual warfare is when African American soldiers struggled to be noticed and considered as human beings by offering themselves as fighters during wartime.

These were times when men of color faced a firestorm of prejudice in eras erupting in racial unrest. White men openly abused them with bitter impunity as they fought gallantly in segregated armies that left many of them maimed or killed. Each generation of Blacks had the same motivation that went beyond patriotism, and into finding some niche for acceptance as men in America. Generational traditions of demonstrating bravery on a battlefield in foreign countries in order to gain parity with White America have plagued the hearts of Black men from war to war. I have read accounts of my ancestors. I have spoken with veterans who confused battle cries with weeping for their rights as American citizens. All wanted to be counted as viable contributors and equals in "the land of the free and the home of the brave."

During World War I, African American soldiers in the 9th and 10th Calvary and the 24th and 25th Infantry, four segregated units were greatly respected by other "colored" people. It was deemed an honor for Black soldiers to serve in the army because many were initially refused the opportunity when they volunteered. This was due to the discrimination that blighted military service for men of color. Then, a quota system was introduced, and Blacks were allowed in the army in limited number. President Woodrow Wilson declared war against Germany April 2, 1917, and immediately it was recognized that White soldiers could not go into battle alone. All men between the ages of twenty-one and thirty-one became a part of the draft system. The Draft Board, being exclusively White, required Black draftees to tear off a side of their registration cards to identify their race. There was an influx of Black men serving on the front lines, particularly if they owned their land because the Draft Board targeted them first and foremost. In the bigoted south, Black men were often arrested as draft dodgers because postal workers, who were always White, refused to deliver their draft notices. The upside of Blacks serving in World War I was the idea that their commanders should also be Black. This was not due to any equality on the part of the War Department. It was due to the stereotypical notion that a prevention in chaos within the "colored" army meant having them answer to their own kind.

World War I knew no braver hero than a 5'4" slightly built soldier affectionately called "Black Death" because of his military actions. Henry Johnson, a rail station porter from Albany, New York, joined the 369th Infantry Regiment in Manhattan. The men in this unit were known as "The Harlem Hell fighters." Segregation during Johnson's service did not impede his "courage under fire." Since the American army was segregated, Johnson's unit served under French command. While he and a fellow soldier were standing guard on the front lines at midnight on May 15, 1918, Johnson and his Negro buddy, Needham Roberts, found themselves caught in a heated battle by Germans who were determined to drag Roberts into enemy camp. Bullets exploded upon the two men, many of them reaching their targets. Both men wounded by gunfire from twenty-four audacious German soldiers seemed destined to meet their doom. Johnson, armed only with one rifle and a knife, shot and killed four of their attackers, then after running out of ammunition, wielded his blade injuring the remaining twenty who then retreated. Forty years of requests from congressmen who believe Henry Johnson deserves America's highest military award, the Medal of Honor for his actions have gone unnoticed. Former New York State Democratic Assemblyman, Jack McEneny has led the charge for many of those years. Johnson received one of France's highest military honors, la Croix de Guerre, but in America, he got a chauffeur-driven ride in the New York parade. There were no awards and no military benefits. The tenacity of several congressmen brought Henry Johnson the second highest military medal, the Distinguished Service Cross, in 2003, but few soldiers in the history of American war have accomplished what he did single-handedly.

Although a five-year statute of limitations for recommendation for the Medal of Honor had long passed, in 1918, or even 1923, Henry Johnson lived in a Jim Crow bubble. It took eighty years for Congress to officially recognize his actions, and for many other unsung Black heroes, it will never come. After the war, Johnson went back to his job as a rail station porter; however, his wounds from the war weakened him physically, and his reception at home tormented him psychologically. Wounded, impoverished, and discouraged, he turned to alcohol. He died a depressed alcoholic pauper at the age of 32 in 1929. A few congressmen continue to fight for a posthumous Medal of Honor for Johnson, hoping the five-year statute would be ignored given the racist circumstances under which he fought. Albany, New York continues to remember his legacy with two memorials, a street and a school named in his honor. The ultimate award for his brave actions has continued to elude him for nearly a century. In 1991, a case was made and won for Army Corporal Freddie Stowers of Sandy Springs, South Carolina, who became the first Black military man to receive the Medal of Honor for his bravery in World War I.

Corporal Freddie Stowers, a squad leader in Company C, 371st Infantry Regiment, and 93rd Division took charge in a battle in which the enemy appeared to surrender. Once their actions were determined to be a ploy, a tremendous battle occurred. Corporal Stowers, with only half his troops left to fight, overshadowed by German soldiers, charged his opponents while crawling gravely wounded on the ground. He beckoned his troops to continue the fight even as he took his last breath avenging the deaths of those who were fallen by the hands of the enemy. Even though he lost his life saving the lives of others September 28, 1918 during World War I, it took 73 years before his actions were given merit by the American military. It might have taken longer if he, like Henry Johnson, had not lost his life on the battlefield.

It took 52 years for seven Black World War II veterans to receive their Medals of Honor. During a ceremony on January 16, 1997, President

Bill Clinton placed the award around the neck of one tearful survivor of the war, Vernon Baker. The other six were posthumous. It was the first time that men of color were honored for their courage during that war. Baker personally obliterated two German machine gun camps and was the leading commander in the destruction of two other hidden traps. He also successfully led his troops through enemy mine-fills in battle, then drew attention on to himself and away from his wounded unit so that they could be safely evacuated from a war zone. President Truman presented twenty-eight white soldiers with the Medal of Honor, omitting the heroism of Black soldiers who were equally valiant in their actions. President Clinton said during his speech honoring Vernon Baker and the six other deceased veterans, "Now and forever, the truth will be known about these African Americans who gave so much that the rest of us might be free." It was a freedom they could not experience on American soil.

Regardless of passing time, God holds the timetable, the calendar He marks for the retribution of tormented souls. Even when it appears that injustice will continue to rein supreme, He fortifies the confidence of his children by demonstrating the beauty of justice in due time. His mercy is never lost or delayed, but timely for the highest purpose of all concerned.

The 761st Tank Battalion, an illustrious group of Black fighters, known also as "The Black Panther Tank Battalion, "led many of General Patton's soldiers into battle during World War II. When Patton rescued and relieved the soldiers in the Battle of the Bulge, the 761st tankers came in to protect an infantry and foot soldiers. They were called the "n" word and many other derogatory names. They were there to protect these white soldiers, and of course gave their lives to protect them, but it did not make any difference. These were the first African American soldiers to fight in the brutal front force of World War II. While other White soldiers served no longer than two weeks on the front lines, the Black Panthers, as they were called, were there for 183 consecutive days. Their contributions to World War II were so valuable, they changed the mind of Gen. George Patton, who believed Negro soldiers to be intellectually inferior to Whites. One member of the group became a famous historical baseball player, Jackie Robinson. Jackie Robinson did not see overseas combat because in August of 1944, he was arrested, and court martialed for refusing to go to the back of an army bus driven by a civilian at Fort Hood. Three years later, after his acquittal, he became a baseball champion for the Brooklyn Dodgers. It appears that God had another assignment for Mr. Robinson; one of biblical and historic purposes.

There were Black soldiers from World War I and World War II who were lynched while dressed in their uniforms. There were cases when tankers were being trained in Louisiana and after they finished that training, they were to move to New Jersey to prepare to go overseas. While traveling through Louisiana, the train had to be blacked out; all the shades pulled down. Black soldiers wanted to know the reason. They were told "because we're going through a part of Louisiana. If white folks saw you on this train in uniforms, we don't know what would happen." They were leaving their homes and going over to fight, and perhaps even lose their lives. It should be noted that there were Caucasian soldiers who were equally as disturbed about tent of Blacks, but even when there is a spiritual interruption against the injustices of the masses, the majority opinion overrules the soulful debate against offenses. Often, groups form a personality that is separate and apart from that of individual thinkers. Following the crowd is one of the fowler's greatest weapons against God's children. Prejudice is a byproduct of following the upbringing and socialization from generations of non-thinkers.

These were times when men of color faced a firestorm of prejudice in eras erupting in racial unrest. They were openly abused with bitter impunity as they fought gallantly in segregated armies that left many of them maimed or killed. Each generation of Blacks had the same motivation that went beyond patriotism, and into finding some niche for acceptance as men in America. Generational traditions of demonstrating bravery on a battlefield in foreign countries in order to gain parity with White America have plagued the hearts of Black men from war to war. Everyone wants to be counted as viable contributors and equals who have a reason to exist. It is that need that beckons the devil and allows his antics to penetrate hearts, minds, and spirits. Most people would rather die in order to demonstrate their value and purpose for living. When that purpose is removed, then it is possible to visibly see the light grow dim in a person's eyes. This occurs when people are relegated to invisible creatures, non-existent, unimportant, null and void.

Many people have discovered that the people who adored them when they were doing well will ignore them when they have fallen into the abyss of hard times. Generally, at a time when a person is most vulnerable, when friendship and kindness would provide much needed treasures for the agonizing journey that erupts like a volcano is desert wind, is the exact time when the phone stops ringing, the door stops chiming, and nobody remembers your name. Whether it is disease, job loss, sudden financial dilemmas, loss of reputation due to error in judgment or by indiscriminate fate, a fall from grace is never a graceful fall. There will be very few people who said "I love you" whom you will ever hear from again. You have been as discarded as yesterday's garbage, and it shows.

A close friend of mine whose work was exceptional is an erudite in her own right. A beautiful yet humble woman, she discovered how audacious her friends and sorority sisters could be. Their jealousy plagued her like shadows of vultures keeping vigil over their prey. She had contributed millions of dollars in equipment, a structure that was a source of pride for the company, and countless hours and years of painstaking diligence to the job and to the company. Suddenly, one day management decided to redirect their focus and brought in some new managers to oversee their vision. This "new vision" was actually a suggestion made by my friend during one of the executive board meetings. One of the new managers was a woman, a sorority sister with whom my friend had confided and assisted during many hours of need. Instead of the woman protecting my friend's position with the company, she set her goal towards eliminating her and making her a target of distain. When her mission was accomplished, the people my friend assisted during her twenty-year tenure vanished. The sorority "sisters" who once expressed their allegiance to her spoke in whispers and hushed tones.

It is not easy to overcome the painful process of elimination. Just as the Black soldiers chose to fight in wars when they were not invited, the battle that rages is actually in the heart. Value is often seen as a commodity that is purchased by grinning confirmations and banal conversations of paper people who can only show one side of their true nature. They often hide the remainder of their dimensions behind the fear and trepidation that their weaknesses and insecurities might be exposed. Fact is, we all have weaknesses and insecurities, but when you are willing to allow them to be viewed, along with all of the human frailties that are common to everyone, the honesty and integrity of the experience draws the human spirit closer to that of the Divine. Life is not a contest where the winner is awarded a prize for wealth, popularity, and the trappings of this world. It is a process, a journey that leads from one destination point to the other, with wisdom and understanding as the great reward. The fact that there are people with whom we once broke bread, vehemently prayed, shared our most compelling secrets and confidences, who have deliberately cast us inside their barrel of disposable encounters can be devastating. But God has a way of weeding our garden so that we are not harmed beyond what we can bear. "No temptation has overtaken you that is not common to man. God is faithful, and he will not let you be tempted beyond your ability, but with the temptation he will also provide the way of escape, that you may be able to endure it." (I Corinthians 10:13)

We are invisible warriors, carefully chosen by the Father to endure the hurts and pains that come from walking in His shadow. Forgotten in our times of trouble by some but endowed by the Creator to pick up our cross in hours of need. We know how to carry our cross because our Savior, Jesus Christ taught us before we were the size of a marble in our mother's womb. After the burdens of crucifixion come the resurrection of a new life, a new purpose, a new goal, and a new song placed in our hearts by the Lord. Weeping is a part of the journey. It is the rain that washes away the hurts from the past. According to scripture, we can we assured that "joy cometh in the morning." Often our detractors cannot fathom how the person who was sinking in the mire of uncertainty can suddenly arise from the devil's foot. Every time a crisis competes for your faith, understand that a blessing is not far behind. Do not watch the clock or a calendar to await the impending promise of restoration but understand that we have a God whose watch carries impeccable time. Let His will be done in His time, and you will see that He is not finished with you or your circumstances, yet. He is using them for His glory and to demonstrate His power in a world filled with camouflaged motives and earthly desires. When the spirit is wanting and cries to heaven seem to go unheard, know that the Lord never leaves or forsakes His sheep. Sometimes, we must rest in the midst of the journey, lick our wounds, and silently walk alone through the pitfalls of life. It is during these times, I remember and sing one of my favorite spirituals, "Whatever my lot, thou hast taught me to say, it is well, it is well with my soul."

You Can Survive

If you can piece together your dreams when
they've been shattered by oppression
If you can release your sadness in tears without drowning in depression
If you can walk upright through storms and kneel when clouds are gone
If you can smile in times of trouble, and pray when nothing is wrong
If you can run the race of life with God as your wings
If you can look to the treasures of heaven
rather than earthly material things
If you can put aside your trials, and forget about troubles
If you can aid someone else when they're battling through struggles
If you can lift someone up when you are feeling down
If you can face a difficult task without wearing a frown
Then you will find the Divine peace and joy that make you feel alive
And there's nothing that can happen to you that you cannot survive.

"I can do all things through Christ who strengthens me."

(Philippians 4:13).

CHAPTER FOUR

The Stain on Man's Soul

Thomas Paine wrote "These are the times that try men's souls"; however, it is not only men's souls that are tried during these economically challenging times. It is their values, their morals, their scruples, and their boundary lines when it comes to acting and reacting with integrity and honesty. Too long have denizens of this society suffered endless indignities, unreasonable business decisions and a blatant devaluing of the human condition for the sake of dollar signs. These currencies have become the signs of the time. The elderly are often ignored by those who have become impervious to their innate Christ-like spirits and find themselves infiltrated by the forces of mundane math. Even some of those who once took an oath to save all lives are adding and subtracting the worth of human existence based on the benign summary of years equated by birth certificates. The summary of age is often used as the measuring stick for providing the equation for human worth.

During the winter of 1961, an elderly couple decided to have a dinner and movie night. There had been so much discussion about a new film starring a handsome new Hollywood leading man, Warren Beatty, and the fetching child star who was now a young beautiful woman, Natalie Wood. Splendor in the Grass promised to be a moving tribute to the sanctity of virginity, true love, and horrendous heart break. The elderly couple, Mark and Marion Drake, enjoyed every morsel of their seafood dinner, even the hard fried hush puppies that got caught in Marion's dentures. The movie proved to be as much of a tearjerker as it had been described by critics, but it had been a good evening for entertainment. Suddenly, Mark stumbled grabbing his chest. He began grunting and crying out in a whisper to his startled wife, Marion, that he needed help. The owner of "The General" Movie Theater rushed outside to assist the couple with Mark and his medical dilemma. A physician was called, and he immediately drove to the Drake's home and diagnosed Mark with a myocardial infarction, in laymen terms, a heart attack. The movie theater owner, the doctor, neighbors in the small community, family and friends gathered at the home of Mark and Marion Drake to determine how to sustain Mark's life and assist Marion with any needs she might have during Mark's recuperation time. It was the early sixties, a time when humanity was generally wrapped in the Divine; one single spiritual umbilical cord uniting feelings of pain, illness, and misfortune. As British author and poet John Donne's famous statement, "Any man's (dilemma) diminishes me because I am involved with mankind." We were all involved with mankind, feeling the angst of a slipped step, a gasp for air, and a skipped heartbeat. Age was seen as a respectful mounting of benign and beguiling experiences, often adorned by the silver in thinning locks spray painted by the culmination of mistakes, mysteries, and the malevolence that grows out of living. The wisdom that arose from mouths creased by tests and testimonies was once hungrily devoured with by gratitude to those who were generous enough to share. Some paths were less travelled, and some lives were miraculously saved by the golden words of an older man or woman whose anecdotes about choices and consequences were reviewed in a moment of weakness.

More than fifty years after the incident with Mark and Marion, one of their descendants found himself in the grips of an unknown illness that was stealing his breath and pounding through his chest. His arms flew sporadically through the air in the view of his children; one of whom left the house immediately because she had to "pay her bills." Later, she would reveal to one of her siblings who was devastated by what could have become a tragic scene that her father was "getting on her nerves" so she "had to get out of there." The fowler has worked diligently with his subjects through the years. He slithers insidiously through minds, shaping thoughts, and camouflaging his motives with desires for a cushioned comfortable existence. Desires for the safekeeping or care of others dissipate like the fading smoke on a used match. When the passion for painless dissolution from the spirit that unites souls becomes a difficult task, the second strike ignites a spark that severs our celestial bond. We begin to disconnect from others, those who were once familiar spirits, and become independent contractors of our own dubious world. We ignore the fact that our most common connection is that of family, one whole unit birthed by one Father. The umbilical cord is cut, and a new creation is born; one known as apathy.

Apathy morphs the mind into a mantra designed to enhance the destruction of the Divine Spirit that once resided inside mankind. "It's all about me," is the silent and spoken directive. That chi, the balance between the positive and negative forces noted in Chinese culture, appears to be the driving force behind conclusions defining the human condition. It has become the medicinal cure for societal ills. The impoverished are often viewed as lazy rather than bruised by the misfortunes of an ambiguous circumstantial charade. There were slaves who toiled in the blaze of a scorching sun and into the bitter sting of brutal winters who were only relegated to dining on unwanted organs from pigs, which they turned into delicacies. So, it is with the dilemmas of the faithful.

When bullets turned a prayer vigil into a tumultuous tragic murder scene, family members and members of the historic Emmanuel African Methodist Episcopal Church in Charleston, South Carolina, called upon their Christ selves to interpret and forgive the bigoted youth whose actions created a prism of pain for their community and the nation. The horror of an innocent peaceful communication with God transforms transformed into turmoil spewing from the eruptions of hell. A congregation was collectively mediating for those unable to attend the weekly devotional, welcoming an unidentifiable face based on the symbiosis of presumed like spirits in an environment designed to call upon the Divine. At first glance, the kinship between Dylann Roof, the unsuspecting gunman, and the prayer team at the church had to be in Divine order. Even Roof admitted that sometime within those sixty dubious minutes of battle between good and evil, between God and the fowler, the net of faithless confusion draped over his mind by the enemy began slipping. He almost decided not to riddle his darker hued brothers and sisters with the malicious metal of hate that seared through their flesh, ending their physical lives and wounding his immortal soul. The fowler's snare snagged an unguarded moment of spiritual clarity; yet released the power of a loving God whose breath of forgiveness soared through hearts like the winds of heaven across the fabric of Christianity.

Many actions and reactions tend to underscore the privilege associated with "free choice" donated to human beings by God as a birthright. We can choose to tap into the primal fleshly response to adversities and those who administer them, or we can choose to reach inside the breath that gave us life and cover ourselves in the protection of His truth. "Then the Lord God formed the man of dust from the ground and breathed into his nostrils the breath of life, and the man became a living creature." (Genesis 2:7).

It has become an era when the dark destroyer confounds the minds of his spiritual victims. No one is immune to his sudden attacks of injustice and cruelty. The kind are considered weak and oblivious to survival skills; therefore, they must be eliminated because. they are construed as detrimental to evolution. Business people, both men and women have reconstructed the architecture of their souls erasing the "golden rule" for a more self-calculating evaluation that revolutionizes the traditional theories associated with values and principles. Regardless of the hardships that show a panoramic view of poverty, foreclosures, sickness, and unemployment, some are committed to their corporate hearts, which nearly always bleed green. The dark integrity of some is so dense, it forms a shadow over dreams of having "the simple life "a life of real purpose.

Kindness is a symptom of a holy infested heart. The human eye is blinded to the vision of good because the face often camouflages the intent of its owner. It is not always easy to distinguish between friends and enemies, particularly in a sea in deception and evil. The bible defines evil intent as seven abominations or signs that go far beyond the structure or contour of a face. "A proud look, a lying tongue, and hands that shed innocent blood, a heart that devised wicked imaginations, feet that be swift in running to mischief, A false witness that speaketh lies, and he that soweth discord among brethren." (Proverbs 6:17-:19). Just as God can identify His children, Satan knows his seed. The outside view of both descendants is not easily recognizable. The bible gives us a hint as to how to determine the offspring of the Lord. "Yea shall know them by their fruits." (Matthew 7:16).

Clarence appeared to be a pleasant man who resided in the south in a nice house in a pleasant middle-class community. He had recently become a widower and was mourning the death of his spouse when his neighbor told him about a job repairing a home in the area. A jack-of-all trades,

Clarence readily accepted the job as handy man, and fixer extraordinaire in the home of a single woman, Vanessa who was perceived to be a work-a-holic. The neighbor and friend who recommended Clarence to Vanessa attempted to make a "love connection" by advising that Clarence was a "good catch." Clarence was a light-built man with a deep voice, but he appeared to be guarded and slightly shy. After a few weeks of working on her house, Clarence began talking to Vanessa about his past. She began to realize that when he spoke, his words were somewhat slurred as if he had imbibed a bit. Since they were not exchanging or sharing cocktails, Vanessa began to worry that Clarence had some kind of a medical condition.

One afternoon while he was working at the house, he stopped to talk. His red tinted eyes and wobbly gait were symptoms of a loss of sobriety. Vanessa was a little taken aback because Clarence was described as a church going man who made some previous errors in judgment in his youth but had paid for his sins and was ready to walk a tighter spiritual rope. His demeanor had always been respectful, even quiet and a bit pious, during the brief time in which Vanessa knew him.

"You don't know what I've been through," he said in a strained voice. It was true. Vanessa did not know Clarence's history and actually thought it rude to pry. She listened intently while Clarence stumbled through his revelations.

"You don't know what it's like to be a big-time pimp soliciting the services of teenaged girls, then taking their money to buy tailored suits and nice rides." Vanessa thought it was a bit too much information; however, everyone has a moment of confession. It is actually considered to be "good for the soul." No one is perfect. Everyone has something they have done for which they are haunted, including church going Christians. Vanessa took this into consideration, even though the pimp thing was a little unsettling to her spirit.

"God forgives us no matter what we have done," Vanessa said reassuringly. "Forgive yourself. That's not your life anymore. Make your new life your testimony to others who believe they have committed unforgivable sins. Tell your story and let others see how a person can change," she advised.

"You don't know what it's like to beat a girl when she can't account for the money, she owes you from the tricks she's been with," he continued as if he were in a confessional trance. "It's really all right. At least you are sorry for what you did back them. Now, you attend church. You've given your life to Christ. God has forgiven worse sins," Vanessa continue her efforts to comfort the grieving man. "Yes, but you don't know what it's like to kill a man." This was the ultimate confession. Clarence began sobbing uncontrollably, but when Vanessa attempted to console him, he made unwanted advances that made him seem disingenuous. She realized he was probably telling the truth about his exploits of young women, but the smirk on his face and the muted sly spirit that appeared in his eyes painted a picture of a man possessed by the power his sins brought him. Reliving them seemed to be more of a joy than a sorrow. Vanessa realized that her assessment of the situation could be unjust, but the fact that Clarence chose to come to her house inebriated signaled a flirtation with impropriety that seemed to remain in this man's heart and soul. Then, the lunging at her while she was simply trying to interject some spiritual compassion led Vanessa to believe their "relationship" would bear bitter fruit if she had chosen a friendship with him. It is imperative that we keep our eyes open, our mouths closed, and our ears widened to hear the wisdom of the Lord when we are interacting with the wounded. There will be opportunities to allow our spirits to shine, objectively without judgment, on the misguided efforts of fractured souls who innately know better, but do not choose better. In other words, "the spirit is willing, but the flesh is weak."

Lynette had a quick-paced gait that demonstrated her multi-tasking talents in the hectic world of the media. Television, and print are all her specialties, with a particular emphasis on public relations, as the company required. As a sixty-year-old veteran of the public relations industry, she reminisced about the days when struggling newcomers would receive constructive advice from the "old timers." It was advice that allowed her to slowly climb a corporate ladder filled with the footprints of those ahead of her, and the handprints of those who pushed others behind the treacherous slope of corporate America. This was a different era when some newcomers worked harder to discard the old regime rather than enhance their own entrepreneurial skills. Those who believed they were being kicked to the curb changed their conversations from dreams of the future to emotion-charged stories of the past.

Lynette Bacon was filled with anecdotes; some cautionary tales, and other amusing remembrances of scenes from a life filled with professional and personal triumphs and trials. She realized that through our triumphs we come to understand our trials, and through our trials we fully perceive the definition of our triumphs. It is like a twist to a well-known phrase altered and used by my father; "Experience is the best teacher" if you can survive the experience. It is the survival that brings the triumph; a lesson learned by both the wise and the weary. Through the years, Lynette discovered her journey through the maze of the former, which brought her to the ultimate destination of the latter.

It was what some would describe as a coincidence that brought Lynette to the public relations industry; a random call led to an unusual opportunity for the then youthful African American woman. Donned in her small sized department store best, and an afro comparable to that of the then notorious rebel Angela Davis, she walked into an interview with some of the people she recognized from industry reviews. "Why do you believe you should work here at the number one agency (in the market)?" asked a successful executive in his strongest baritone voice. "I am certain with all of my unmined creative skills, I can contribute to the advancement of this agency," she replied confidently. The interview was a hit with the suits as well as the veterans who recognized the potential in this young aspiring professional. She worked hard through the years, writing and producing award-winning campaigns. She put words in the mouths of her well-established colleagues and mentors and headed most of the agency's most prodigious projects. Nearly every segment of the work viewed by the masses brought rave critiques. Wages were meager, but steady; and the compliments kept her motivated and content about her career in the future. The first ten years were amazingly productive, even lucrative by the standards of an ambitious young woman who was reaching her creative peak. Many of us realize as time so swiftly passes like windblown dust, for every peak there is a valley. Some valleys are inevitable, God's plans for human changes and growth that evolve like seasons seeping through the hands of nature. Others are premeditated like the primal erosion of a predator's vengeance. Some call it the "dark side" of emotions; a turbulent relentless nemesis that corrupts the heart and pollutes the mind. It is like a net that traps within its threads the spiritual mortality of faith- filled believers.

Opportunities to enhance her talents and skills were inevitable during the initial season. The company had a "jump in and swim" philosophy, which allowed her to showcase her abilities. Her work was well received internally and externally. She found herself thrust in the role of writing more. Writing and producing became her greatest talents and fulfillment.

As one year plunged into another, Lynette worked energetically on all the major agency assignments. She decided to leave this prestigious job in pursuit of her dream in a larger market. Recognition was elevated; then a sudden shift in company ownership changed everything. This meant a shift in personalities, values, concerns, and regrettably, a change in the manner in which Lynette's work was reviewed. "I need to see all of your work while you are creating it. Why did you use that word? I don't like that shot. I want you to change the concept." Back-to-back conflicts and criticism with the new team of leaders created confusion and a cacophony of negative voices. Lynette found it difficult to understand that often it is in the best interest of corporate leaders to ask the tough questions, reexamine the work of the past in order to assess the pulse rate of the future. As many of us who have lived beyond the point in which we are called "youth" can attest, life is a seasonal journey. There will be years of plenty, and years of lean. Just as Joseph sought God's interpretation of Pharaoh's dream in which seven lean cows ate seven fat cows, and the seven lean heads of grain devoured the seven more robust heads of grain, there are predictors that indicate we are reaching the conclusion of one season and the beginning of another.

Each season is drastically different, just as we see from this parable in which Pharaoh is being warned about the seven years of plenty and seven years of famine. Ecclesiastes tells us that we should prepare for the inevitable seasons of life. "To everything there is a season, and a time to every purpose under the heaven..." (Ecclesiastes 3:1) As composer and singer Stevie Wonder puts it melodically, "Nothing and no one goes unchanged." The bible further states, there is "A time to get, and a time to lose; a time to keep, and a time to cast away..." (Ecclesiastes 3:6). When we are ill prepared for these necessary changes, it can set the stage for spiritual homicide.

Lynette's request for meetings to discuss the work, her attempts to change the writing to suit the new corporate style, and her desire for professional objective conversations with management were all met with inexplicable silence. Words can often become daggers that pierce the soul and leave its victims wounded and dismayed. The lack of words or totaling ignoring a person as if their very essence is meaningless can be an ominous force that depletes confidence. Coworkers generally embrace the climate set by corporate behavior, and many began to ostracize Lynette.

Although it is inherent within the corporate community to examine, evaluate, and decipher the work that represents the company, there is often coldness in the corporate body for those who do not fit into their collective image of what a worker should be, how an employee should look, or how the profit bottom line may be impacted by a multitude of factors. This is often reflected in the manner in which supervisors communicate with their "underlings."

Contrarily, there is a spiritual bond we share as human beings; an invisible umbilical cord that stretches throughout every soul. It is this bond that allows us to feel beyond our own existence, a baby's innocent smile, a puppy's sweet face, and the hot bitter tears that glisten from the eyes of a distraught person. These are all poignant parings of hearts that are emotive and shared. When the chills of self-gratification, the impulse to concentrate solely on the things that apply to individual satisfaction outweigh combined interests, the result can be dehumanizing. Lynette discovered the sting of verbal and non-verbal interaction with her new supervisors to be denigrating and spiritually destructive. Immediately, she began to question her worth not only as an employee, but also as a human being. An aging overachiever now stressed by the countdown on her career, too old to start over and too young to retire, craved a gentle good-bye, and faced an implosion against her worth.

If you have ever been in this position, you know what happens biologically. Your heart pulsates, beating rapidly and sending heat throughout your body. Your palms become slick with sweat inching aimlessly toward the digits in your hand. Your throat becomes a desert, and your mouth becomes pasty thickening your tongue. Swallowing is like an Olympic event bringing a gag through your vocal cords. The enemy uses this as an opportunity to whisper negative thoughts about the dilemma. "Maybe you are too old, too black, too female, and too fat. You will probably never rise from this moment of rejection. After all, who cares about you? Others are able to rise to the top and stay there, but not you. What does that tell you about how God feels about you?"

There will also be those loquacious "friends" and co-workers who will feign empathy and sympathy while gossiping about your plight with every opinionated person. A re-examination of spiritual communication leading to the defining moment is imperative if you want to regain the power of truth. There will be days, months, years, sometimes even decades when seasons of financial, emotional, health-related, family dysfunctional, incarcerating drought seem to linger. Consider Nelson Mandela who spent twenty-seven years behind bars in his efforts to change the horrific racism of South African Apartheid. February 11, 1990, he walked from his imprisoned tomb reaching across racial lines to blend racial ties and become the first Black President of South Africa four years after his release. Mandela had nearly three decades of an unchangeable environment, yet God was continuously preparing him for his greatest season and finest hour. He forfeited bitterness for fortified faith.

It is a grueling formality to go step by step in slow motion away from familiarity and into that unknown nebulous tomorrow. If you have ever known rejection, you understand it is like a groping web that traps, and then releases your spirit in a downward spiral of uncertainty. Lynette Bacon is now a published author and poet, currently residing in the south. Her dismissal was perceived as an agonizing event in her life because of the manner in which she envisioned it, but there was a spiritual resurrection. Survival is inevitable once we learn and trust that God has a plan.

United by the Spirit

What color is the rainbow and why does it exist?
It creates a sacred circle embellished colors on its list
The darkness of the clouds provides a sacred hue
Where light merges with musical tides playing right on cue.
Together, the mixtures of heaven created for soulful blend
Burst from the womb of the sun embracing end to end
And God in His enduring love creates the melting pot
Born from the Father's Heart divided we are not.

"Thou hast proved mine heart; thou hast visited me in the night; thou hast tried me, and shalt find nothing; I am purposed that my mouth shall not transgress."

Psalm 17:3

CHAPTER FIVE

Liberty and Justice for All?

Every breath of life is filled with the prospect of phenomenal fate, moments of angst and augmented favor dwelling in the same space in dueling times. Understanding the distance between happiness and hopelessness is like measuring the air as it blows across bristling trees, soft and faint. Powerful in its ability to change the direction of a journey, destiny is often defined by the small thoughts and heated words that develop into escalating actions. Imagine having dark skin, and being sentenced because of this act of nature, being this product of the production of a Higher Spirit claimed by cultural reference as the Infinite God Almighty, to be the odium repulsed by the lighter hued peoples spewed by the mouth of the same God. It is the knee that pressed against the bulging veins of a prostrate Black man on the dirty hard asphalt of apathy by a man whose mission was "to protect and serve." It is the echo of a jail cell that once held of woman of color stopped for a traffic violation, whose neck was later discovered dangling from the transformed tomb by her jailor. It strikes with the passion of bullet holes that penetrate the awakening startled flesh of a young woman whose crime was sleeping in her own bed and having some knowledge of a person who might be eluding the police. Anxious law enforcers recognize later that the suspect they were seeking was in custody and attempts by the boyfriend who shared her space to protect her would be arrested for his efforts. Death often comes quickly when you are Black and hunted by those in blue.

Racism begins as a thought, a demented fragmented delusion of grandeur and an immeasurable comparison of color. The darker the hue, the more embellished the prejudice, a pre-judging of the very nature of a being. Black men and women have struggled with the distinction between their dark skin and their decreasing rights as citizens. Each person of color, with few exceptions, have their personal stories of injustice and inhumane treatment based on a tradition of oppression. Those who have risen against the tide of despair have sacrificed their peace for the freedom of all humanity. It is only when the flow of justice washes over the human rainbow that those who are ensnared by the demons of bias can be released from the flood of racism.

There is a dark eclipse that is infiltrating the light of justice and equality. It creates a color-coded nemesis for people of color. Add the midnight mist of bigotry, stir in the egos of the un-slaved who have lassoed rings of hatred around the necks of rainbow hued Americans for more than 400 years, and we have the classic ingredients for the storms of pugilistic upheaval.

Black Lives Matter, too, particularly when they are marching through the shades of trees that once bore the fruit of their beloved ancestors, who died only because God chose to paint their skin darker, curl their hair tighter, and arm them with more tenacity and courage to endure the "slings and arrows of outrageous times." Even Lady Justice seems to high-five the avert and catastrophic activities of hood-hiding dark souls whose egos only allow for one master color; regardless of the kaleidoscopic of beings created by the Lord.

Those who have not experienced the venom of prejudice cannot comprehend the vulnerability that comes with innocent existence in an environment of whimsical assault.

Regardless of the appearance of social, economic, or employment status, the mere fact that a brown or black person has reached a perceived "plateau" in the booby-trapped ladder of myopic "success," there is no protection against the historic indelible imprint of racism, not only in the deep south, but wherever a person of Black heritage resides.

Shadows in the Midnight Sun

Ebony silhouettes ignite a light
A candle blazing in the heart of midnight
While shadows engulf breathless sighs
Into the darkness my soul lies
Before I drown in the mire of hate
Bloody, yet bountiful the sun I await.

"Fear not, for I am with you; be not dismayed, for I am your God; I will strengthen you, I will help you, I will uphold you with my righteous right hand."

Isaiah 41:10.

CHAPTER SIX

Shadows in the Midnight Sun

Being clothed in permanent black skin from birth means struggling for equal stakes in the race for human dignity. When Cordy Tindell Vivian was born on July 30, 1924 in Howard County, Missouri, his destiny was written in the blood of his ancestors whose limp bodies wreaked in pain from the malady of white supremacy.

The only child of his parents, Robert Cordie and Euzetta Tindell Vivian, he began his formative years under the guidance of his mother and grandmother after his parents divorced when he was six years old. His mother and grandmother migrated with young Vivian to Macomb, Illinois. Neither Howard County Missouri nor Macomb, Illinois could be called a metropolis in which the midnight son would be expected to shine, but he did. It was selected by his matriarchal duo because of its non-segregated education base. It was their dream that the brilliant brown boy would someday become the upstanding leading man who could bend the bars of racial incarceration for people of color and allow them to escape their wretched limitations.

After Vivian graduated from Macomb High School in 1942, he attended Western Illinois University in the same city. His star shone brightly as the sports editor for the school newspaper. Ever the curious and mercurial warrior, Vivian left his leadership role at the school to become the Assistant Boy's Director at Carver Community Center in Peoria, Illinois. It would be a fortuitous move because it was there that he met his love mate and wife, Octavia, who also worked at the Center.

They were married in 1952. He later received his Bachelor of Arts degree from Georgetown University in 1997 and his Doctor of Law (JD) degree from Columbia University in 2000.

Octavia Geans Vivian was a talented and creative writer, whose spirituality merged instantly with that of her husband. She earned her degree from Eastern Michigan University in social work and maintained her dutiful connection with the church throughout her life. During their fifty-eight-year union, the couple welcomed and raised six offspring: Denise Vivian Morse, Cordy Vivian, Jr., who died in 2010, Kira Vivian, Mark Evans Vivian, Anita Charisse Thornton, and Albert Louis Vivian. Octavia Vivian was the first scribe to pen a biography of Coretta Scott King; aptly called *Coretta*. Understanding the indelible ink that marks history, Octavia Vivian collected and organized all the pertinent documents that told the story of SCLC and how it advanced the American Civil Rights Movement.

A progeny of exceptional women powered by faith; Dr. C.T. Vivian discovered the power of non-violent protest in 1947 when he participated in Peoria's first luncheon counter sit-in to break the belligerence of segregation. It was during this moment; he heard a still small voice that whispered a beckoning call to the ministry. Vivian realized only heaven could cure the vicissitudes of chaotic racism that festered within the Black experience.

He enrolled in American Baptist Theological Seminary in Nashville, Tennessee, the alma mater of John Lewis. It was 1955, an era of massacres and missions, a year when the toll of bigotry hung over the heads of innocent black youth, like Emmett Till in Money, Mississippi. It was a time when the heady stench of racism burned so hot, it left a brand on the soul of America. Holding high his religious upbringing, Vivian believed he could find biblical answers that could quench the tempestuous fires of hatred. That year, he formed a bond with other Nashville ministers who founded the Southern Christian Leadership Conference (SCLC). Together, the band of spiritual warriors took up their sedate swords and led organized, trained students into a non-violent battle against segregation and racial inequality in Nashville. The group congregated to form the first Civil Rights march for the Movement in 1960.

Before that first march, in 1959, Dr Vivian and others in the Movement were taught non-violent training from the strategy of Mahatma Gandhi's philosophies. On April 19, 1960, Cordy Vivian and a fellow cohort,

Diane Nash put their lessons to work at Nashville's City Hall, where they challenged the mayor. Ultimately, they succeeded in getting Mayor Ben West to publicly confess that racism was "morally wrong." The same year, Vivian became one of the leaders of the Students Nonviolent Coordination Committee, better known as SNCC. He joined the courageous Black youth as a part of the Freedom Riders, who endured a blood bath while attempting to desegregate bus facilities that were to be legally available to people of every color. The prospect of reaching stoic hearts wearing white hoods, and boisterous bullies in blue uniforms was daunting and filled with violence. The Freedom Riders endured unmerited arrests, pummeled heads, swollen eyes and burning buses. When the Riders were sent to Mississippi's most notorious prison, Parchman, Vivian was beaten so badly, he nearly lost his life. However, like all things that are cemented by the Highest Spirit, his notoriety was fodder for promotion. After the Parchman debacle, Dr. Martin Luther King, Jr. requested his presence on the Executive Staff of SCLC as National Director of Affiliates.

The couple moved to Atlanta, Georgia when Dr. Vivian decided to take the job offered by Dr. King. Octavia Vivian became the first African American Deputy Voter Registrar in DeKalb County Georgia, while she continued to pave the road for Dr. Vivian's impossible mission to erase the hate of hood wearing combative Christian Caucasians. Two years later, Dr. Vivian made national news when he stood on Selma Courthouse steps to make a speech during a voter registration drive. Blood oozed from his mouth when the Sheriff pulled his arm back with clutched fists and struck Vivian in the mouth, displaying his transparent racism on television. The incident and other abasements of the Civil Rights journey were chronicled in Dr. Vivian's book, "Black Power and the American Myth," the first of its kind detailing the Movement. He organized and became board chair of the National Anti-Klan Network in 1979. He founded the Black Action Strategies and Information Center BASIC, an information center on diversity and multicultural training in which he worked with his son, Albert. The two won the first Lifetime Achievement Award in Atlanta Business Chronicle's inaugural Diversity and Inclusion Awards.

2011 was a momentous year in the life of C.T. Vivian. President Barack Obama honored him, along with his fellow iconic Civil Rights veteran, John Lewis with the Presidential Award of Freedom. His beloved wife of fifty-eight years died, leaving him a widower, but his sacred trust in God carried him through the murky seas of life's continuum. On July 17, 2020, Dr. Cordy Tindell Vivian exchanged his blows, beatings, and belittling for a peaceful stroll in Paradise with his wife and his friend, John Lewis who died on the same day. While they swam through the belligerent seas of racism with lifeguards filled with faith, their fear drowned in the uprising of their courage. Both pioneers understood, when you walk through a storm, or fight the foe of bigotry, you never walk alone.

Good Trouble

The cradle of the Civil Rights Movement is filled with the souls of sacrifice emerging from the womb of inequality. Their plight is carefully formed by a Higher Power who arms them with a dedication that is unmatched by mere mortals. Congressman John Lewis was born with the shield of tenacity in one hand, and the banner of freedom in the other on February 21, 1940 outside of Troy, Alabama. His parents, Willie Mae and Eddie Lewis, wrestled with crops in the blistering bigoted fields of Alabama's torrid winds of black despair. Livelihoods were seasoned with salty color bias, yet there remained dignity peppered in the making of a good sharecropper. Their son, John, the third of ten children, was solicited to assist with the work. Poverty was as common as cotton. Troy is a small town in the bowels of the south, where dutiful black hands caressed the growing prickly crops of each season. One brilliant mind raced from Jim Crow's fiery fields into the promise of a crisp cool valley filled with freedom.

Washed in the struggle with sweaty brows, dodging the propelling saliva of Caucasians spurned by the inevitability of legal change, Lewis became a pugilist against injustice in the abyss of discrimination. He realized quickly that his response to racism could lead to an early death. However, John Lewis was not moved by the mortality that hovered over his cause, he was propelled by his inborn spirit to contour his body and meet the violent rage of racism with all its horrors. Beyond the depths of physical limitations, walking through the torrential storms of shark-tooth German shepherds, maniacal taunts and threats, he was greeted by law enforcers who were neither lawful nor protective of Blacks. John Lewis took the reins of redemption for an oppressed people and held on relentlessly to the last fiber of his being. Weeks before he succumbed to his malignant state, propped up by emotional protestors on all sides, his waif-like body painfully took its final weakened steps for human equality during the walk against the violent murder of George Floyd.

"It made me so sad. It was so painful," Lewis told "CBS This Morning." "It made me cry."

It would be just another in the mounting tears that flowed like a pounding rain from Troy, throughout the perennial protests the inhumane neglect and persecution of ebony hued peoples. Segregation was like a gaping wound in the lives of Black people. When Brown vs. the Board of Education in 1954 offered a significant change in public schools, establishing the illegal practice of school segregation, Lewis's school was not affected. This brought alarm and disappointment to the justice minded scholar whose loving family life did not match his stymied existence beyond his parents' doors. Lewis took up his gauntlet and set off to accelerate the power of his purpose, to exclaim that "all men are created equal." Then a voice rang out in the middle of his battle against bigotry, one that inspired him and many others. Dr. Martin Luther King, Jr.'s mesmerizing words echoed throughout the nation, and gained volume in Montgomery, Alabama. His Montgomery boycott ignited the innate passion in John Lewis to change callous hateful cries into peaceful humanitarian unity. He matriculated at American Baptist Theological Seminary in Nashville, Tennessee, where nonviolent protest became his greatest mission. Painfully rising above his mother's tears and his father's fears, he organized lunch counter sit-ins in Nashville; then, joined other indomitable young leaders for the Freedom Rides of 1961.

The riding rainbow of youth traveled to segregated facilities at bus stations in the south to assure that Supreme Court's decision to desegregate was being accomplished. Primarily, most of these were students willing and ready to face a sea of snarling white faces stifled by hatred and uplifted by bull whips, tear gas, and Billy clubs. Bloodied, bruised, yet unafraid, John Lewis forged on to help Dr. King plan his honor bound March on Washington that beckoned millions.

When Civil Rights became law in 1964, there was still no change in the tyranny against Black people within the prejudiced white society.

Lewis became chairman of an organization established to address the consuming chaos between rights and ridiculous rancor, particularly in the establishment of voting rights for Black citizens.

March 7, 1965, an infamous day of irreputable brutality, was appropriately entitled "Bloody Sunday." John Lewis, the new chairman of SNCC, the Student Nonviolent Coordinating Committee, led 600 students in a peaceful quest for voting rights across Edmund Pettus Bridge in Selma, where the march began its fifty-four-mile odyssey to Montgomery, Alabama. The group faced the violence of troops whose pounding to their heads and lacerations to their bodies landed John Lewis and another heroic Civil Rights icon, Hosea Williams, in a hospital. Regardless of the blood splattered on the asphalt, it was this tyrannous incident that prompted a hurried pace for the Voting Rights Act of 1964, a major victory for minorities.

Every battered mile he traveled; John Lewis blazed a trail on the battlefield of historical balance for subjugated people of massive dark complexions. Every blow to his body, every accelerating heartbeat from the fear of assassination, every tear that formed a path down his face, contorted by the pain of physical destruction built a foundation for change.

After mourning the assassinations of Dr. King and Robert Kennedy in 1968, Lewis picked up the torch. He married the love of his life, Lillian Miles Lewis, the same year. Their nuptials continued from 1968 to 2012. Lillian Miles taught in Nigeria, then volunteered for the Peace Corps for two years prior to meeting her husband. During years of constant illness, she continued to work hard to assist her husband in his fight for racial justice. She insisted on hiding her debilitation from the public. Her goal was to allow John Lewis to continue his charge toward human rights for tortured Blacks. On New Year's Eve, forty-five years to the day she met John Lewis, Lillian Miles Lewis closed her eyes in permanent slumber. The couple has one child, John Miles Lewis, a musician who has not completely shut the door on political aspirations.

In 1970, John Lewis became Voter Education Project Director, and was able to register millions of minorities for voting. Public service was always his spiritual destiny. He won a seat on Atlanta's City Council in 1981, and five years later, he became one of the nation's most popular congressmen, representing Georgia's 5th District. During his thirty-four-year reign, he elevated the standards of congress, and was immediately named "The Conscience of Congress." Along the way, he garnered many prestigious accolades, including the NAACP's Spingarn Medal, John F. Kennedy "Profile in Courage Award" for Lifetime Achievement, the Presidential Medal of Freedom, presented to him by the first African American President of the United States; an honor that brought an emotional impact to a life filled with dreams deferred.

"When we were organizing voter-registration drives, going on the Freedom Rides, sitting in, coming here to Washington for the first time, getting arrested, going to jail, being beaten, I never thought — I never dreamed — of the possibility that an African American would one day be elected president of the United States," he said proudly after President Barack Obama's election in 2008.

Fortunately, President Obama's election was an impossible dream made possible by the Highest Authority. The life of John Lewis, a remarkable testament to faith and infinite endurance was fated for generations to follow. Lewis, a consummate erudite, unable to go through the doors of a library because of his skin color, won the National Book Award for the third installment in a comic book series, "March: Book Three;" the first time a graphic novel had been honored.

As the collective years bleed one into another, the glory days of heroic intent for the cause of righteous works will form a legacy of hope for those left inside the bleakness of discouragement. Pioneers like C.T. Vivian, another fallen warrior of the Civil Rights Movement, and Congressman John Lewis will create strong threads in the fabric of justice and equality for all. The path they paved is filled with the stain of blood from the wounds of injustice and uplifted by the tenacity of undaunted spirits. When John Lewis closed his eyes and released his body from the earth into the heavens, he knew he had fulfilled the mission that catapulted him from a small town in Troy into the now bleeding hearts of America. John Lewis vigorously fought through repression, now he can finally rest in peace. His life was filled with trouble, and his message reverberates throughout the dark halls of injustice. "It's alright to get into trouble…but make sure it's good trouble." Trouble that extends beyond the boundaries of prejudice and discrimination could end a movement and begin a destiny.

There are stories of such men and women, victimized by the new order; those who survived with the aid of their faith, others who were decimated during their journeys. The world often misses those who succumb to more overt natural disasters like the gusty chills of a raging storm, or the crackling and crumbling of trees that ultimately tumble to diminish cities and demolish communities, all great catastrophes; however, few words are spoken over the victims of spiritual storms that form like tornadoes from the mouths of those who leave spiritual, emotional and even physical human splinters in their wake. The world continues to evolve, but all too often its evolution leads to darkening abyss between whites and black forming the grey palate of the human condition. All the symptoms of this new societal order led to abuse.

Free Dumb

Free Me
Free Choice
Free Imbibing
Free Voice
Free Risks
Free Pills
Free Disturbance
Free Still?
Free Hurt
Free Pain
Free Theft
Free Bane
Free Spirit
Free Fun
Free Deception
Free? Dumb!

"A fool gives full vent to his spirit, but a wise man quietly holds it back"

(Proverbs 29:11)

CHAPTER SEVEN

Free Dumb

We all have free will. It is a spiritual license given to all by God, but some take their free will as an opportunity to destroy. Freedom becomes a clash of words and actions used like weapons to annihilate others. Freedom can digress into "free dumb" because the instigator eventually succumbs to their remarks. Time can be a ticking bomb hiding in the deep recesses of words that return like a boomerang. Whatever is released by the tongue comes back with a vengeance bringing delight or destruction to the sender. One of the most provocative liberators of an abusive tongue is self-induced drug overload. Overindulgence in drugs, both prescribed and illicit, taken with an alcohol chase can be dangerous to the mind, body and spirit.

Frank Carlton was a blonde-haired blue-eyed fiftyish executive who had reached the high ranks of his profession. Noted for his straightforward no nonsense speaking, he was both feared and revered by colleagues and subordinates. His family tree boasts of professionals who worked diligently to provide the family with more than the mere necessities of life; however, his parent's recent illnesses drained their savings. Frank inherited the work ethic of his parents, but not their diplomacy, values and ethics.

It is written, it takes a whole village to raise our children. Today, more than half of that village are victims of the internet, invisibly cavorting with pedophiles, murderers, rapists, thieves, and demonic forces beyond detection. Good people raise their children in a God-fearing manner, but it is alarming how the Dr. Jekyll - Mr. Hyde personalities emerge from world enticed selfishness. This predicament is born from the seduction of potential wealth, fame, and the life-and-death power over fragile things. Frank enjoyed the pleasure of it all, especially the ability to play God in the lives of others. His narcissism was fueled by excessive drinking mixed with prescription drugs. His family also factors into the equation because there is a history of malevolence that began in Frank's youth.

According to relatives, his favorite words are 'I have to take care of me. God bless the child that's got his own." It is a mantra that has followed him since he was a boy growing up in a large city with a small-town personality. Although neighbors were affable during those growing years, few of them were likely to become involved in family tribulations.

Frank was treated like royalty as a young boy racing through the community on his ten-speed bicycle. People remember his long yellow hair bouncing across the Greek features on his angelic face. Few knew that behind closed doors, Frank was a child who manipulated his parents, siblings, and anyone he could in order to achieve his goals. The bicycle was a gift given to him by his parents to taper down his tantrums, and to prevent him from crying relentlessly until someone acquiesced to his demands. He was an average student, applying himself only to his thespian abilities. Frank once struck a student in the head for giving him an unfavorable critique regarding his acting prowess. He was described as a mean little kid by students; however, his teachers saw a more subdued and quieter boy.

At the age of twenty-one, he married a woman he had known for only a few months. It was a secret ceremony unknown to family and most friends. His wife, a stout good-hearted woman with a contagious laugh, was often on the receiving end of his voracious tongue lashing. The moniker he gave her was "Hefty Refty," blending her name, Refiel, with a reference to her weight. Often during arguments, he would blast in her ear, "Nobody wants you! You're fat and ugly!" Her self-esteem plummeted, while his libido led him from one frivolous affair to another. He spoke to his conquests via telephone all night long while lying next to his wife in bed. "These are just friends," he would say in response to her complaints. Less than six months later, he would live with, and later marry, one of those friends, bringing her into the home he once occupied with Refffy, a nickname most people called her. Two years later, his second wife wiped out their joint checking account, and left him for a man with whom she was having an affair.

Through every incident and season of his life, Frank remained the outspoken executive with the egregious nature and hair trigger temper.

The only living creature for which he had any affection was his dog, Marty Boy. When Marty Boy died, it was the first sign that Frank had emotions that paralleled those of other human beings. He spent thousands of dollars trying to save his beloved pet, but the prognosis was bleak from the beginning. The death of Marty Boy brought an increase in his pill and wine consumption, and more demeaning obscenities to those whom he believed he could control.

One of the things Frank appears to be recycling is a constant fear of loneliness. Although he spends most of his time creating misery for others, he is committing spiritual suicide. His inner tears spill from his tongue in profane ways, but his heart bleeds with the imperfections of a child lost in the wilderness. Frank anesthetizes his feelings by plying drugs through his system and drifting into an emotional coma. Frank's rages and consumptions are symptoms of inner warfare against himself.

His childhood, although idyllic by the standards of many, was the precursor for future abhorrent behavior. Temper tantrums rewarded with gifts; money given so generously that the gesture signaled entitlement all tend to produce the guilty pleasure of outrageous behavior without a sense of conscience. Frank understands the difference between right and wrong, and his parents brought into the household a customary set of values by which the family should live. Through his eyes and mind, this value system applied to everyone but him; yet he recognized the imbalance between his behavior and the anticipated and accepted conduct of others. The more his thoughts perused the blatant litany of missteps he made, the greater the battle between spiritual contentment and worldly amusement. The remedy for this condition means relinquishing power over those he considers as weaklings, and the control that comes from the substances that placate his actions.

Spiritual resurrection continues to occur for the people he attempted to destroy with his words and deeds. His parents are thriving and surviving through sources that include his long-suffering sister and community outlets. Others have been able to recuperate by returning to their faith and thereby reestablishing their commitment to go beyond a world of mere existence and into a spiritual life.

Frank continues to drink, take pills, exert his authority over others, and denigrate his public and private image. Although many have reached out to him to save him from himself, the prognosis for success remains pending. Frank suffers from dis-ease; a condition that breeds discontentment with the inner self. Many prayers rise to the heavens on behalf of Frank. Believers understand that life breeds hope, which means there is a possible return on the prayer investments that continue in Frank's favor. Meanwhile, he is the personification of self-determination gone awry, adding to the premise that free is not always liberating. It can also release a demonic false sense of joy that ultimately proves to be "dumb."

Mystic Missions

Has the shadow come to greet me, or I to greet the shadow?
Am I the bait for the abyss of the mind, or a
greater and more conquering foe?
Should I wander through the deadly spell,
or wait for a heavenly remedy?
Will I hear the echo of celestial sounds, or
adhere to the whims of the enemy?

*"Yea though I walk through the valley of the
shadow of death, I will fear no evil."*

(Psalm 23:4)

CHAPTER EIGHT

Mystic Missions

Spells and witchcraft are practiced all over the world. Those who believe they are the targets of some abhorring magic often grimace at what is deemed to be the effects. It is the belief in some cultures that people using instruments, potions, candles, and other paraphernalia have the power to control the destiny of their subjects. Others cling to the theory that these are merely mind-altering games devised for sufferers to victimize themselves.

A proliferation of access to the powers of spells can be found in periodicals, magazines, books, and websites. One website has a one-year guarantee on revenge spells and curses developed through the purchase of specific amulets. Another website defines the categories of spells and witchcraft, stating that the traditional version gives the person casting a spell the ability to control both body and property. These are evil spirits that are posed to attack through incantations. Rosemary Ellen Guiley in the 1999 article, "Candle Love and Magic," believes lighting a certain colored candle will bring desired results. The bible speaks of witchcraft and evil spirits, confirming the existence of its ancestral legacy. "The acts of sinful nature are obvious…immorality, impurity…witchcraft." (Galatians 5:19). Often, Christians are the willing participants in spell casting, citing the need for husbands to return, employers to be punished, and former friends to be penniless. According to Minister Nydia in her 2012 article, "Witchcraft Spells among Professing Christians," it is "an obsession with control and domination that drives some people to seek counsel and incantations from a paranormal source. Spells are often seen as the ultimate answer to avenging the mistress of a wayward husband."

Mayla Ellis was a former custodian for a reputable company in the Deep South. She appeared to be a consummate loner with ambition that stretched beyond her duties. As she walked somberly down the hallways, her blossoming cheeks hung down toward the soiled mop inside her rolling bucket. It was late, and darkness crept through the windows like a black curtain silhouetted around her rotund body. The effort to take each step was obvious as each bulging leg struggled to leave the floor. Anyone watching would take a second glance in wonder of what menacing grip held her captive to the emotions and thoughts that seem to overtake her.

Mayla clumsily fiddled with a ball of keys as she opened a locked office door. After emptying the trash, she closed the door with the hem of her soiled uniform caught half in and half out the office. Watching her from my dim office, I hurried from my desk scattering piles of disorganized papers across the seat. 'Let me help you, 'I said in a quiet non-judgmental voice. Her head fell into her chest as she murmured. "I don't know what's wrong with me." I studied her heartrending posture and said, 'This can happen to anyone.' While reassuring her, I reached for the heavy metal bracelet she had fastened around her wrist. I opened the door and pulled the tip of her soiled uniform from the door's grip. We exchanged names and I tried to lighten the mood. "I've always heard this office is haunted." I noticed my giggle was returned with silence; then Mayla jumped in a nervous shiver, grabbed her bucket, and began to run. Calling behind her and telling her that I was only joking seemed to accelerate her pace. Feeling the pangs of guilt sweep over me, along with the crawling warmth of embarrassment, I followed her to the Break Room where she sat sobbing. I immediately took the chair next to her and softly patted her back.

'I don't know what is going on in your life, but if I can do anything to help, please, please let me know.' I thought that was a stupid joke about the haunting. Interrupting me through a garble of sobs, she said "I am haunted!" My mind raced with thoughts like, 'this lady is probably a mental health patient who is starting over. You struck a vicious nerve.' Or maybe she just got out of prison where they told ghost stories about how the prison was inhabited by dead inmates. As I combed through the litany of reasons why she believed she was haunted, Mayla raised her head and looked into my eyes with water still cascading around her cheeks. It was the first time I realize how pretty she was. Her glassy eyes sparkled through the light brown haze in a geyser of sadness. Her heavy flowing hair was wavy and jet black against her olive-colored milky skin. 'Doesn't this woman know how beautiful she is? I wonder why she is so incredibly serious,' I pondered.

"I really don't talk to people too much, "she said. "Please don't tell anyone what I am about to tell you. For one thing, they won't believe it." I explained to her about a book I was planning to write about the disturbing occurrences in some lives. 'I want to interview you for the book. I promise not to use your name,' I said. Mayla's eyes seemed to penetrate every human and spiritual covering as if she were staring at my soul. Her voice was grim from crying, yet gentle and sincere. "I want somebody to know what happened, but I don't want them to know it's me."

After assuring her of anonymity, she began a story that is fascinating and scary; the type of anecdote I had not heard since my days in Catholic school where we openly discussed demonic activities. "I know you wouldn't believe it now, but once upon a time I was fairly pretty." 'You still are,' I said, quickly trying to avoid the beginning of a self-deprecating monologue. "No," she admonished. "Listen to me. I was thin, but I was what the old folks call fast. I'm thirty-two years old, but I know I look fifty." It was true in one sense, yet a hint of hidden youth would emerge then suddenly leave like a picture under a strobe light. The story was going to be good. I could feel it in the goose bumps that popped out raising the hairs on my arms. At this point, I excused myself to grab a legal pad and a pen.

"At sixteen, my mother warned me that I was growing up too soon. My parents were strict. We went to church every Sunday, and I wasn't allowed to date until I was sixteen. That was when I met a man twice my age. He was a powerful businessman with a wife and three kids. He promised to give me things I never even knew existed. I didn't know anything about a Rolex watch, and Gucci shoes. He even gave me money to pay the mounting bills in the house."

I was struck by how intelligent Mayla was and wondered why she seemed so self-effacing. The tears streaming down her face seemed lighter but flowed steadily.

"He did what he said, and we had a full-blown affair." She paused to wipe the tears from her eyes and blew her nose on an old pocket rag. I listened for the next round of confessions like a child waiting for a monster to appear in a scene from a horror movie. Any upcoming revelations were bound to lead to one devastating and eerie moment of change. "My mom's bills were paid. I wore beautiful designer clothes, and drove a red corvette fully paid by my man, or at least that's what I thought," she continued in a hoarse voice. "I was a church going girl, sang on the choir. Didn't smoke, drink, or fornicate before meeting this man. I was living what I knew because that's what I was taught growing up." Somehow, I knew this story was heading towards an unhappy ending, but I was in no rush to get to it. The details were fascinating as each layer smoldered somberly from her lips. 'So, what happened to make you feel a married man would be the right person to date?' I asked gingerly. "He gave me things. Nobody had ever given me expensive gifts, taken me on trips, bought me a car, paid my mother's rent…" It was the quintessential story of an older man looking for a temporary trophy he could discuss with the boys at a bar, boasting about in whispers in a clandestine hover. 'His wife found out, right?' My patience was constantly vacillating between suspense and getting to the bottom line.

"A lady called me one day while I was on someone else's cell phone because mine all of the sudden wouldn't hold a charge." 'How did she know the number?' I asked in apprehensive curiosity. "This is the part of the story you won't believe. She said she had been to a witch who told her my name, where to find me, how I looked, and even what cell phone I would be using. "At that point, I am unsure of whose eyes enlarged more; hers or mine. My attempt at pacifying her with logical solutions was obviously unsatisfactory. 'No offense, but I any amateur detective could give out same information.' I rationalized. Mayla began shaking her head rapidly in disagreement. "You haven't heard it, yet. Back then, I had a mouth on me. I told her I had her husband and he loved me. I threw in some choice profane words. I went on to say she might as well give him up and let us go our way." I wondered what kind of person this was. Dating someone else's husband, cursing his wife, ignoring his three children, one of which was close to her age; what morals did her parents really instill in her and why was she betraying those teachings? She answered each question as if she could read my mind. "I was young and dumb; thought I could do whatever I wanted to do. You can easily forget your upbringing when someone is dangling your dreams in your face." It is the proverbial trap that snares people, even those much older than Mayla. A man in this case, a woman in others, making offers few would refuse; however, the idea of consequences dissipates like the first smoking ember from a burning house.

"I hung up and kept talking to my girls," Mayla said breathing erratically. "I thought I got her told. Now she knows not to bother me again. Then, my phone rang again. It was her. She said 'Listen carefully. You just made the biggest mistake of your life. In your entire lifetime, you will not be able to undo what you have done. You are pregnant with a little girl. I could tell you her name, but that's too much for right now. Yeah, my husband is obviously the father, but have you ever heard of Helen Keller?" Mayla coughed nervously, and then paused. "I said 'No!' She yelled and said 'Look her up! That's what you and my stupid husband have done to your child!' Then, she slammed down the phone. It really sounded as if she threw it up against a wall or something." Mayla described how the blood drained from her face, and how her frightened appearance alarmed her "girls" as she called them. When they questioned what was said, her response was "Just another crazy woman trying to hold on to the man she lost." I took a long deep breath, then a sigh. After a few poignant moments of silence, I said 'Wow!'

She continued without acknowledging my reaction. "I didn't know I was pregnant. I hadn't missed any periods, but my breasts were a little sore. I went to the Health Department, got a test, and found out I was four weeks pregnant." By this time, I was both intrigued and empathetic. Here is a young woman whose entire life changed because of a manipulative man, a revengeful angry wife, and an innocent child who was being introduced as a pawn in a maniacal game of adulterous chess. "I cried and cried and cried. I didn't know what I was going to tell my mother. I wasn't thinking about how I was going to tell him." Was your mother supportive?' I asked engagingly. "Is that floor?" She responded indignantly. "The first thing she said was 'I told you so.' The second thing she said was 'You gotta get out of my house.'"

Where did you go?' I was now taking copious notes as we talked.

"I went to him and he got me a motel room. He paid for it, but I worked cleaning up the rooms at the motel so I could buy little things I wanted. I hadn't told him about the baby yet; just that my mother had kicked me out of her house." I took a pause and excused myself to go to the lady's room. I needed to process all this seemingly convoluted

Stephen King drama before Mayla reached the finish line of her tale. My mind kept playing back the images of a young teenager who was playing with fire; a suave lothario, a vindictive wife, and a witch's spell that seemed implausible. I walked into the bathroom perusing my notes and almost wishing I had not pressed this young woman into telling me this sadistic story. Now, an innocent baby is introduced into the scene. I kept quizzing myself about whether I should hear the remainder of this twisted supernatural melodrama, but I was hooked.

When I returned to the room reviewing my notes, Mayla was wiping down the microwave feverishly busying herself with the nightly chores. She hurriedly gathered paper towels, carefully placed then in the dispenser, and appeared to be tossing around her previous words with pensive pathology. I gazed silently at each jerky move only to see a wounded spirit with an aura of darkness surrounding her. The darkness was not emanating from the alleged spell, but from the rumbling of a tornado swirling around the guilt of an adulterous affair; one that produced a child she believed she had damaged.

'What happened to your child?' The question jolted Mayla from the tedious tasks and back into the world she had been describing. Groping for a chair to sit down without making eye contact, she managed to plop heavily into the seat, and then stare aimlessly out into the window framed shadows.

"My daughter is beautiful, smart, and sweet." She paused and took a deep sigh. "Blind, deaf, and unable to speak. I cannot bring myself to say that word 'dumb.'

I clumsily sat down to join her at the small chrome table, trying to avoid making eye contact before my beckoning tears formed. There was no prompting necessary for a follow up statement. "Bill, my so-called man, found out I was pregnant. He promised to divorce his wife, marry me, and move to Montana, of all places.

When my baby was born with all those defects, I got another call, this time on my home phone." This story had become too surreal, and with such intimate details, I was beginning to feel a little intrusive.

"It was his wife, again. Hadn't heard from her in eight months. She said 'How do you like me, now? Consider me as your personal prognosticator.' I had to look that word up to find the insult." We both released a small chuckle that broke the sullen mood of the moment. "She said 'Now Bill will leave you alone to raise your poor child, and you will learn a lesson.' It's funny how she never really cursed me out or anything." Mayla seemed almost grateful for this small courtesy. I kept thinking the lesson would be to never date a married man, although this witchcraft stuff was making me extremely uneasy.

The lesson appeared to have a loftier meaning. "She said 'When the flesh is strong, the spirit becomes weak.' Then she just hung up the phone. A few days later, Bill came by with some flowers, a check for $5,000, and a warning to leave him and his wife alone." Mayla jumped from her chair as if to get that kicked to the curb feeling off her backside. I watched her intensely as she grabbed her mop and soaked it in sudsy water. 'Do you believe this was all the work of a witch?' I asked trying not to sound incredulous. Mopping as if she could scrub the truth into the dingy floor, she said "I don't believe anybody is gonna believe this story, if you decide to write it." I did not either, but it was too fascinating to ignore. 'Did this really happen to you?" I asked with my voice automatically elevating. "She told me I'd lose my looks, get fat, fall on hard times, and I have done all of those things." 'But have you prayed?' I asked wondering if she had any spiritual acumen left from her church going years. "All the time, now. My pastor is one of a few people I shared this story with, and he said I should repent. God will forgive me. Then, he gave me this bible quote that I recite all the time. 'No weapons formed against me shall prosper, and every tongue that rises against me shall be condemned.' (Isaiah 54"17) She referred to her upcoming GED classes with an illuminatingly bright smile overtaking her face. Although her first pregnancy left her barren, she and her daughter have a special bond. She offered another powerful verse on a small piece of paper used as a bookmark inside her pocket-sized bible. "God's got my back. I know I did wrong, but Jesus died to make it right."

Fourteen years after what she mysteriously referred to as 'the visit,' Mayla did not hear from Bill or his wife.

After thanking Mayla for her story, our two-hour conversation ended. While mentally deciphering all the details of this tainted tale, I watched Mayla go into the Ladies Room to mop the floor. She waved out of the door and said, "God bless." Through the remaining few months of her employment, we passed in the hallway with a courteous, yet distant "God Bless" and a wave, but we never reconnected.

Mayla could have created this story based on a need for drama. It could have been an imaginary vision to protect her guilt-ridden conscience concerning her daughter's condition, or it could be the truth. Perhaps, the wife she described and admittedly never met was a karmic haunting brought on by a breach of spiritual and moral ethics. Everyone takes a driving test before operating a vehicle, perhaps Mayla was going through a spiritual test, and her vehicle was her faith.

The fowler comes in many forms; temptations, ability challenges, the negative spoken word that targets the heart and tears the soul like a demonic spell cast upon the subconscious of a fragile mind. It is only when we recognize the relentless stalking of the enemy and its intense pressure on the human spirit that we can adequately hear the voice of a Higher Power echoing through the noise of absurdity.

A Walk through the Fog

Beyond the stream of breathless tears
My spirit rises above all fears
And, in the hour of dark dismay
My soul is refreshed as I pray
Bless me Father while I weep
For each humble moment awakens my sleep.

"We walk by faith and not by sight."

(2 Corinthians 5:7)

CHAPTER EIGHT

A Walk Through the Fog

Each moment in life is a mystery unfolding like a fruitful blossom exposing strengths and frailties; then releasing itself into oblivion. There is no limit to what the human spirit can endure. Beyond the horizons of the imagination, and beneath the pit of fiercest pain, there are no boundary lines. Caution signs flicker inside the inner realm, yet our eternal compass can falter. Some experiences albeit negative in the traditional sense can seduce the spirit and present a rite of passage for the person who is destined to be its subject. Some events can give even the most prodigious life traveler a new perspective on the lack of hegemony that exists on this somewhat whimsical journey that begins at birth and has eternity as its ending.

January 2, 1998 began like a joyful opening to a season of encouragement for Missy Martin. After seven years of living through street congestion, the hurling and hustling of her television career, and empty corners of a nonexistent social life, Missy finds solace in freelance writing gigs, long telephone conversations with friends, action-packed movie dramas, and science fiction shows like "Beyond Belief: Fact or Fiction." It appears to be the simple life, filled primarily with writing and producing promotional spots for the News Department at a reputable competitive television station a highly populated market. However, on this Friday, a vacation day taken after New Year's Day, life would take a remarkable turn.

It was a relatively frigid day, particularly in the south, and Missy wore her most comfortable soft bathrobe while she made one of her trademark dishes, spaghetti with meat sauce and chicken livers. While the water vigorously boiled, she dropped in the spaghetti when the doorbell rang in her quaint, cozy townhouse. The laughter she shared with a humorous friend on the phone was put on pause while she questioned the persons on the other side of the door. "Who is it?" She asked with giggles trailing off her gleeful voice. "It's the police! We're looking for Missy Martin." She quickly opened the door and investigated the faces of two burley officers who resembled "The Hulk" right after a moment of anger. They were six feet seven inches tall, at least three hundred pounds each, wearing stanch stares, and the bluest of police blue uniforms. Their eyes spewed venom as if they were facing a criminal from the FBI's ten most wanted list. Missy's first thought was some prankster from work was pulling a joke. "How can I help you?" she responded in a light airy voice. "Are you Missy Martin?" It was beginning to sound like an episode on the old "Dragnet" series. Even the expressions were identical to the lackluster characters on the show. "I am," she replied, still wearing a silly grin. "We have a warrant for your arrest." After a premature explosive guffaw, it was finally apparent that this may not be a joke. "What are the charges?" She quickly whispered to her friend who was now silently holding the phone. "Are you hearing this?" Her friend responded with great trepidation. "What's going on, Miss?" Missy turned back to the hulk like officers and inquired about the charges. By now, both officers with their towering frames had moved inside her foyer, past her and into the living room area. One produced a paper that showed a copy of a check she had written months ago for a parking violation. He held it in the air with authoritative assertion. "This is the check you wrote for a parking violation." She nodded apprehensively, wondering why it might have bounced, why she was not notified, and when insufficient funds required an arrest. Why did they wait until at 9:30pm and send the two largest officers they must have had on the force? "We don't take checks," the officer said, waving the image of her check in his hand like it was the key evidence in a homicide. The words loomed over her head like an invisible hammer, lowering down softly, raising back, and slamming into the deep recesses of her mind. All she could do is mutter, "huh?" "You better get dressed. We're taking you in," said the less vocal of the two mammoth giants with a smirk on his face.

By now, her disturbed friend on the other end of the phone was nearly frantic wondering what was happening. The officer was brandishing the paper with the copy of the check like it was a fierce weapon. He demanded that she hang up the phone. "They're taking me to jail for writing a good check for a parking violation."

Missy walked slowly up the stairs to her bedroom, confused, devastated, and prayerful that these two men were not a part of some Neo-Nazi group who targeted African Americans living in the area. It was one of only a few times Missy Martin even thought about the race card; noting that there was no logical explanation for burly Caucasian police officers, straight from the casting of a Klansman movie to arrive at her doorstep in the middle of the night over a PAID parking violation. Suddenly, her "blackness" seemed to gleam like blood from the southern roots of her ancestors.

Reflecting on November 1997, Missy recalled the endless bouts with flu that would send her to the store for a variety of cold remedies. Frigid temperatures, fast food, and foolishly few sleeping hours combined to create a less than healthy season for the busy professional. It was one of the biggest television rating periods, which meant a barrage of writing, editing, and production; then changing and re-changing it all. Perfecting the imperfect was prevalent during those periods of viewer seduction, camouflaged as "special reports", and the promotion for it all would be under constant scrutiny. Between nerves and nature, quick stops at the neighborhood grocery were increasing, while parking spaces were rapidly decreasing. Parking on the side near the store's entrance became habitual, but illegal. The only warning of how illegal could be seen mounted on a simple "No Parking" message painted on the asphalt; something that a lethargic woman past her prime would quickly overlook, if her only goal was to run inside the market, pick up a cold remedy, then scurry back inside her vehicle and drive home speedily. It was a ritual she had performed many times before, but this November day would prove to be fateful.

"Don't feel like the lone ranger. I'm writing a ticket for all of these folks parked here." A cheery officer responded to the dismal look on Missy's face when she ran out of the store and witnessed a parking ticket being written for her car. "I was sick, and..." The officer just smiled, handed her the ticket, and bid her good day. Defeated by her own actions, Missy got into her car and wrote a check for the $35.00 infringement. Since there was a mailbox in the same strip mall, she rummaged through her much-disorganized purse, found a stamp, placed it on the envelope, and then mailed it immediately. As far as she knew, that brought an end to the situation. It was not until the two giant law enforcement agents rang her doorbell that she even thought about the parking ticket, or the way she paid it.

Missy put on a long uniquely cut dress that had been designed and sewn for her by a very talented neophyte. It was her favorite because of the look and the warmth of the material. She slipped on her log knee high black boots, and then offered herself to the officers as a passenger in their state vehicle. "We'll have to handcuff you," one said while grabbing her arm firmly and fastening the iron bracelet to her thin wrists. It was as if she were a murder suspect or had participated in a robbery. Their actions almost assured her that these two men were not actually from the police force, but instead were acting on their own; perhaps even representing some racist organization that identified her as their next mark.

The drive from her home to the police precinct was like moving through the darkest tunnel in the world. There were no streetlights that identified the location, and no way could she possibly know the direction in which they were taking her. Her mind vacillated between the anticipation of flaming crosses, irate boisterous people clothed in blood-stained white pointed hoods and garments, to a flashlight in a sparse wooded area with just these two gargantuan boogeymen exercising their perverted pleasure. All scenarios played like an anachronistic nightmare that only those born of a darker hue could comprehend. The blatant injustice that arises from color conscious whites is a script written too many yesterday's ago. Keeping her composure, and reflecting on her days of conducting on-air interviews, she asked the officers' names. "Joe Lindsay and Paul Lowe," Lindsay said gesturing to the brass on his shirt and that of his partner. "And you are *Miss Channel 58," Lowe interjected. Missy's work was conducted behind the cameras. It had been years since her face had been seen in front of a camera; nine years to be exact. She pondered over why the two men were addressing her in that manner. The two men continued taunting her with this new moniker and discussing her colleagues as if they were personal friends, or enemies.

When the police car pulled up to the county police department, Lindsay, and Lowe continued their taunts as they walked into the precinct. They led Missy to a dimly lit room where she was photographed, then placed into a tomb-like glass cell. After contemplating her situation for about an hour, and being joined by shop lifters, inebriated drivers, and other more serious offenders, the hour was multiplied by sixteen. Finally, Missy was chained to another inmate and ordered to board what she called "The Cool Hand Luke" bus to travel to a courthouse miles away from the Police Department. (Cool Hand Luke is a 1967 movie starring Paul Newman as a prisoner arrested for damaging parking meters. He was shackled and transferred into fields of hard labor in a rusty old van). Like Luke's character, Missy was shackled to another prisoner at the ankle, then handcuffed as she rode in what looked like a haunted vehicle. She waited near a courtroom for what seemed to be endless hours in a dungeon-like holding cell, void of ventilation, or even other inmates.

A 9am courtroom appearance stretched past noon while she waited in a breathless tightly enveloped hole devoid of light. It was like a round incubator, closely sealed on all sides with no human traffic edging near it, and no one checking on her health and safety. She prayed in faith wondering the reason for this extreme reaction to a viable form of currency exchange for an infraction as minor as parking in front of a neighborhood grocery store. There could have been many sinister motives, but as a Christian and a believer in spiritual rationale, her mind took inventory of the sins she may have committed, the cruelty she might have caused, or the chaos for which she might have been responsible. There was nothing extraordinary about her life except this moment.

God often allows unjust proprietary privilege over the just, but always for a higher cause. Sometimes, he uses experiences to expose the hidden corners of corruption and evil in people and in organized systems. He selects chosen children whom He has groomed for the experiences. Sometimes, the person lives to recount the abuse and enlighten the masses. Other times, they become martyrs for a spiritual cause while the whole world gasps at its own ignorance. The rhetoric of equality provides the base for collective consciousness that enables groups to act. Either way, the open wound of injustice bleeds through the written instructions of commandments against oppression and tyranny. Whether these directives are taken from the American constitution, which was based on biblical principles, or the sacred source itself, the hypocrisy of the heart is not invisible; nor can it remain hidden.

After hearing her story, a judge sentenced her to "time served." An investigation into the matter yielded the fact that no one in the history of the county had ever been arrested for writing a "good" check for a parking violation. In fact, there had never been an arrest for a parking violation period. The magistrate refused to believe Missy was the first. Some experiences are a rite of passage for our spiritual awakening. God does not have to ask our permission to use us to shine light in dark places. It is incumbent upon each person to be prepared because we are all living to achieve that goal.

When we are targeted by the fowler, the attack generally precedes a blessing; a spiritual rejuvenation that renews and restores our being. It does not always happen immediately; however, if we "wait on the Lord and be of good courage He will strengthen our heart." (Psalm 27:14). Even the most devastating of life's challenges that we believe are insurmountable can and will be important life messages that carry us into the next level of our journey. They say more about where we are going and lessen the pain of where we have been. Time may not heal all wounds, but prayer and supplication to God's will can mute the fowler's howl and moderate his effect. When we put our entire lives in His hands, we have no regrets about our todays, and no fears about our tomorrows.

Common Lies

To walk the shores of madness with imprints in the sand
To say you love yourself, but not your fellow man
To taste the bitter tears of saying good-bye
But never touch a heart, and not be condemned to try
Is like swallowing a pea, and watching your belly rise
Puffed up by the small things, impregnated by common lies.

*"A righteous man hates lying, but a wicked man
is loathsome and comes to shame."*

Proverbs 13:5

CHAPTER NINE

Common Lies

One of the most captivating of the fowler's snares is the telling of things that are sensed to be true without a base or fact. The most inauspicious conversations often begin with "Did you know?" These words are often followed by a flurry of condemnations against someone in a circle of friends, family, or a person unknown to the assailing tongue. The information comes with a license to regurgitate a myriad of unforgivable sins allegedly perpetrated by the object of secret gossip.

According to 1857 speaker, Rev. C. H. Spurgeon the fowler (Satan) operates through secrecy. His theory is the Christian or well-meaning person is caught in a net of deception through a near contagious set of forces set up by the enemy. Few people turn away from salacious information concerning someone they believe they know. Lies are the most prevalent tools used by the fowler to destroy the innocent because spinning a tale dripped in drama is a seemingly harmless and entertaining source of communication.

There is always someone who knows the inside scoop on the private lives of other people. Thomasina Jones is one of those people. Often referred to as "the mouth of the south," Thomasina could tell you about a mosquito's cavities before it dined on human flesh. People believed everything she said, and they even thought her knowledge base was so extensive, it would make even the most talented journalist or investigator weep with envy. No one can be accurate about everything, particularly when it comes second and third hand. All of Thomasina's information was "top secret," and could only be relayed to the most confidential ear and sacredly sealed mouth. Most of us know the phrase "don't mention this to anyone." Secrecy is the cloak of the enemy because its discretion quickly leads to indiscretion. Once lies are spoken, they can confound the very existence of a human being. They are deadly mine fields that explode off the breath like a toxic vapor causing human annihilation. They can pierce the spirit and weigh it down like an anchor tied against the heart; moving its victim into a dark pit from which there appears to be no escape.

Thomasina Jones was the bearer of great lies, some she heard from others, and some that were simply embellished for the sake of storytelling. There was one embellished truth that put some of her closest friends and relatives behind bars. Mrs. Jones, who readily revealed the illogical and unproven sins of those in local government, spread unfounded details of a teacher's "misconduct" with a disgruntled student, and interrupted the career of a good worker, then ultimately became the victim of her own words. That is one of the ramifications of talking ill about others. Most of us are guilty of this lashing out against the human spirit. This qualifies as both spiritual homicide and spiritual suicide, for "we reap what is sown" by the seeds that we plant.

Thomasina Jones envied an employment position held by an ambitious woman at a reputable company. When her competitor proved to be more competent, more knowledgeable, and more capable, Jones attempted to get her cohort fired by lying about her work ethics. These fabrications ultimately caused the envied employee's dismissal. Dissatisfied with merely costing the woman her job, Jones embellished the truth about her character to her former employees, thus creating a false reputation that was difficult for the woman to disprove. Later, it was discovered that Jones, even during the time that she falsified information about her coworker, was involved in an elaborate fraudulent scheme that had been under a long-term investigation by authorities.

Thomasina Jones enjoyed the luxurious things money could buy; yet despite her illegal activities and the falsehoods she told to get them, remunerations for her iniquities seemed to elude her. She relished in a quiet Ponzi scheme introduced to her by her often-absent paramour. Revenue for an anemic legitimate business that she tried to maintain appeared to be the only meager measurement for her actions. Unsuccessful at achieving the position for which she attempted to steal from her banished competitor, starting a company of her own seemed the most reliable next step. The business was supported by the money she drew from those she conned into joining the illicit clan of conspirators. After years of an investigation, Thomasina was arrested, along with some unsuspecting relatives and friends on multiple charges of fraud. She was intrigued by the money, of course, but more so by the idea of fooling people into something seductive by the beckoning power of the dark director. This intrigue cost her freedom, but seemingly more important, it shattered her reputation as the omnipotent messenger of hushed woeful tales. of neighbors' woes. The bible states in the book of Job "You, however, smear me with lies; you are worthless …Oh that you would become completely silent. And that it would become your wisdom." (Job 13:4-5).

There is a sadness attached to the untruths that put a crack in consciences and an albatross around the necks of those seduced by its fleeting promise of power. Bigotry and racism are the twins born from the lies of inequality and superiority. Lies are the conquerors of love, dignity, and humanity; for only the purity of heaven can master the blindness that comes from egotistical insecurities. It is the great divide that occurs before the enemy collects a soul, devours a spirit, and makes sacred the emotion called envy.

Often, envy can present a dangerous rhythm of pulsating myths that cause character assassination. This occurs in employment situations where jealousy is the elixir unwittingly consumed by the faint of heart. Surprisingly, in many cases, this competition is between a manager and an underling. If the tenacious subordinate demonstrates a penchant for the work ethic, it can be threatening to someone who has achieved a higher position in the company's hierarchy. Rising through the ranks on the proverbial wings of nepotism and favoritism produces insecurities and paranoia that can serve as a weapon against hard-working optimists. There is a reason why envy is one of the seven "deadly sins." It can kill enthusiasm, promote discouragement, and destroy the very essence of the soul. This new era known as the "Me Generation" is one of the greatest symptoms of the pulling force and temptations that plague the human soul because of the seduction of the fowler. There are many stories of how this turns into temptation, and from temptation into inhumane actions affecting the lives and deaths of its countless victims. Academically, abuse is clearly defined based on the insights of dictionary author Webster, as "a corrupt practice or custom." The medical community, according to The Free Dictionary by Farley, describes it as "any action that intentionally harms or injures another person." Biblically, it can be viewed as "the fowler's snare." The snare of the fowler is analogous to an immoral bird that stalks innocent prey. According to renowned Pastor C. H. Spurgeon in his March 29, 1857 sermon at The New Park Street Pulpit, "Satan is the fowler who betrays unguarded souls a thousand ways." Spurgeon's sermon also explored the changing methods of the devil; describing him as a more sophisticated spirit, a "well-spoken gentleman" who no longer persecutes his prey but seduces them with "beguile and persuasion." Thus, the unsuspecting, or unguarded soul is tempted by the trappings of this world, a fleeting time release that whimsically sucks the life out of its residents. That is the reason we aim for the place of Eternity, a fortress where we will not be randomly evicted but will dwell in a constant state of security with the armed guards of peace.

The Seduced Soul

How deep the wound, how sick the soul
Seduced by night, impaired by its hold
A glimmer of light beckons through the dark
The spirit of a song with the sounds of a lark.

*"Trust in the Lord with all thine heart and lean
not unto your own understanding."*

(Proverbs 3:5)

CHAPTER TEN

The Seduced Soul

The spiritual ear is deafened to the cries of the person in need, and the amplification of personal interests increases in volume until the listener is seduced by the perversion of revenge. There is an adage that states "Hurt people, hurt people," but there is no happy ending to a cycle that defines this adverse behavior. If hurt people hurt people, we are destined to live in a world of constant pain from virtually every person we meet. The theory dictates that once you are hurt, you are predisposed, and rightfully so, to hurt others with impunity. In fact, it is expected. The temptation to harm others is deemed as the normal way of life as if being in a painful state is common and ordained by some invisible power, and it is. The power of darkness that is a part of the fowler's snare.

Temptation is the cornerstone of much spiritual impairment, but so are illness, loquaciousness, envy, vanity, and so many of the demons that attach themselves to our bodies and our minds. We cannot blame others for the clashes that occur between our spiritual and fleshly selves; for as it is written, "the spirit is willing, but the flesh is weak." Plaguing thoughts manipulate the purity of our hearts, imprisoning our wills and creating evil outcomes. So many people close their eyes in regret of their actions, words, and deeds. Apologies have become anomalies rather than conscience-driven reactions to painful words and wounding deeds.

July 17, 2014, Eric Garner, a Black New York City resident is shot and killed by police after selling cigarettes illegally on the street. August 9, 2014, Michael Brown, a Ferguson, Missouri African American teenager is confronted by a police officer who shoots to kill after Brown shoplifts a pack of cigarillos in a store. November 12, 2014, Tamir Rice, a twelve-year-old

Black brandishing a pellet gun is shot within a few seconds of police arrival when a 9-1-1 call requests an investigation into the child's behavior. December 4, 2014, Rumain Brisbon, an unarmed Black father of two is shot and killed by police in Phoenix, Arizona while delivering fast food to his children. White police violence has been a perpetual threat to the life span of African American youth. The shooting death of Amadou Diallo on February 5, 1999 in New York may have sent alarms throughout Black America, but the increase in deaths between unarmed Blacks and white officers appears to have been mounting. Although there are no relevant statistics that confirm that Blacks are the targets of white police violence, there is a legacy of white law enforcers who have profiled, shot and killed Black teens that trends back to the 1950's and 1960's. Civil Rights icons whose lives continue to unfold from the traditions of the Old South understand how sixties law enforcement tactics and those in our current era intersect to form an egregious haunting of continuous police brutality. It should be noted that this does not apply to all law enforcers. There are many who are devoted to the principle of "protecting and serving their communities without racial bias. However, the racial angst in the severely segregated south of the sixties mirrors a practice that has become contagious throughout the nation in current times.

"The biggest difference is the publicity. In the 60's police violence against Blacks was not reported in the newspapers or captured by television video as it is now. The only way we received information about the death of a Black man by a white officer was through the community or a family member," one civil rights leader said. "Now, with technology and the advent of the cell phone, people are better able to see what is happening." Some civil rights enthusiasts recall how they were beaten during their incarceration in at Parchman State Prison in Mississippi during the freedom rides because they refused to reply to officer interrogation with what was then called "the proper response." "We were supposed to say 'Yassah, and Nassah' in order to maintain our societal role. Even saying 'Yes, sir or No, sir' brought retaliation because we were not speaking in the vernacular that was relevant to our race." During some conflicts between law enforcers and black males, officers either declare they were not addressed respectfully, or they felt threatened by the posture, movement, and sounds emanating from men of color fleeing when they heard the commands of the police.

Men of color flee because the color of blue uniforms has become a s lethal and frightening as men cloaked in sheets carrying blood-soaked ropes.

George Floyd was described by family and friends as a low-key common man who prayed with the forlorn and frolicked in the fields with his young daughter. It took one visit to a grocery store in which an alleged counterfeit twenty-dollar bill was passed to find him begging for his life while pinned down in a face first position by law enforcers in Minneapolis, Minnesota. Although Derek Chauvin has become one of the first officers to ever be charged and convicted with the murder of a "suspect" they were taking into custody, his 22.5-year sentence will never bring back to life the father, brother, cousin, and multitude of friends who have visited and revisited the ominous haunting video of Floyd's life ending. The tall athletic Floyd begs officers not to place him in the back seat of his vehicle because he had a phobia. When they finally complied with his pleas, they handcuff him, place him on the ground face down and three law officers delivered a death grip while Floyd cried out for mercy, even soliciting help from his deceased mother. There was no remorse, conscience, humanitarian feelings, no still small voice that reminded them this man was inherently like them. He had a child, siblings, friends, dreams, love, everything they enjoyed in their lives. Nine and a half minutes of torture, and human abandonment caught on tape for the world to view the outrage of depleted spirits and abandoned souls. They may have conquered his body, but his spirit remains in the plaza where people continue to pay tribute to him, in the statues that are erected in his honor, and most of all, in the minds and heart of those who never questioned if God is dead, but instead ask when will His nemesis be bathed in relentless fire, so his stain will be removed from its indelible imprint tattooed on the insidious minds of wavering souls.

When an unarmed young African American, Jonathan Ferrell, who was a former Florida A &M football player was shot and killed a Charlotte police officer, Randall Kerrick on September 14, 2013, the nation took notice. Late in the murky midnight hour, Kerrick approached Ferrell because of a 911 call he received that described an attempt at breaking and entering crime committed by a bleeding black man with a huge physique. Historically, being a large black man appears to be one of the most reprehensible crimes committed by African American youth. Apparently, the size of a black man determines his aggressive nature and is just cause for the use of fatal force by police, particularly when the clock ticks past midnight on dark and deserted street corners. Kerrick says that he warned Ferrell to stop, but the wounded victim of a recent car crash who was looking for some roadside assistance continued to walk. Ultimately, the police officer, with a backup officer nearby, claimed he feared the young athlete was attempting to gain control of his firearm. He believed the weaponless black man was a danger to him and to his partner. There was a Taser gun at his disposal, but the size and demeanor of this injured victim of the night who had the misfortune of crashing his car and walking wounded through the community in question brought fear and trepidation to two armed officers; one who put ten bullets in Ferrell before handcuffing him for additional protection. Obviously, the "suspect" was dead before he was handcuffed. Derrick was charged and there was a trial. The verdict yielded a mistrial with eight jurors voting to acquit and four jurors voting to punish. Later, it was determined that Kerrick would not be retried. Many law enforcers who have shot and killed black people are not convicted; they merely face those who are incensed by the multitude of mistakes that have taken the lives of so many unaggressive darker hued inheritors of prejudice fought by civil rights activists. It will be interesting to see what happens in this case. One move in a positive direction is the fact that someone determined there was a case to be had, explanations to be made, and a life for which someone must be accountable. Freedom riders were arrested due to their non-violent desegregation of bus facilities in the south. Many of our heroic legends of civil rights were struck down by bullets because they believed in the validity of constitutional rights. Very little has changed from those turbulent times in which prejudice against Black men and women commanded deadly force by officers investigating "suspicious activity."

"The bigger the black man, the whiter police officers say, 'I was afraid.' Another Black leader observes. "Bernie Madoff, one of the most notorious thieves in history who stole billions in a Ponzi scheme was captured without being shot. We have serial killers like Ted Bundy, Ricardo Ramirez, Jeffrey Dahmer, and many others who were unharmed during their encounters with police," says another civil rights icon.

There are many correlations between police action now and when the freedom riders and other civil rights workers protested racial injustice during the early sixties. "Protests today include blacks and whites, just as they did during the Civil Rights era and the freedom rides. It is good to see that kind of unity against racial oppression in city after city." One civil rights icon recalls a trip to Cleveland, Ohio fifteen years ago when he was pulled over by a police officer for dubious reasons. Instead of approaching his car, the officer spoke through a loudspeaker and instructed him to get out of his car. "I put both of my hands out of the window and requested that the officer open my car door because of my discomfort with his demeanor and his reason for stopping me. The officer grabbed his gun when he approached my car. After I inquired about a record of our encounter from the camera on his vehicle and demanded to speak with his commander, his tone changed. When his superior, a black officer arrived on the scene, that seemed to dilute the situation considerably."

Fathers and grandfathers of minority youth are giving black males a warning and advice on what to do when they are stopped by police. "I have two grandsons and I tell them to be respectful, keep their hands up locked in position behind their backs where officers can view them. Make no sudden moves, and pray," one African-American male states. He adds that police officers should go through rigorous psychological testing before they are allowed on the streets. For many African Americans who are questioned, then shot by police for "just causes," Lady Justice may appear to be blind, but obviously not color blind. She is peeping through the maniacal creases of a demented demonic cloth; one with a view of different races, ethnicities, religions, lifestyles, colors, creeds, and national origins as targets on a spiritual battlefield.

We remain on the battlefield where biases are like land mines torpedoes that can wound and destroy the spirit of what our forefathers attempted to build. It has been said, "Those who do not remember their past are condemned to repeat it." Every story that maps the course of the journey that leads to now is a reminder of the blessings received through sacrifice and long suffering. The news story regarding the incidents of perceived racism within police departments around the country against unarmed Blacks are disturbing; an anachronism in twenty first century America. Blemishes of bigotry still darken the corners of this evolving nation. These are evident in cities like Ferguson, Missouri where unarmed eighteen-year-old Michael Brown was shot and killed by White police officer, Darrin

Wilson on August 9, 2014. Brown was a young man headed for college, but his brief life curtailed any dreams for his future.

According to an investigation by the Justice Department, there was a long-standing tradition of inequity between police and Black citizens in Ferguson. Unlike in some previous cases, there was a soul searching that translated the rhetoric by members of the inner circle into an exposure of the truth. This demonstrates the slow but steady evolution of the country in establishing justice. The most revealing part of the investigation was exposure to the Ferguson Police Department record, along with the inflammatory e-mails passed through cyberspace within its walls. This excerpt from the Justice Department Report demonstrates the healing that is still needed between racial divides in America.

1. November 2008: An e-mail said President Obama would not be president for very long because "what black man holds a steady job for four years."
2. March 2010: An e-mail mocked African Americans through a story involving child support. One line from the e-mail read: "I be so glad that dis be my last child support payment! Month after month, year after year, all dose payments!"
3. April 2011: An e-mail depicted President Obama as a chimpanzee.
4. May 2011: An e-mail said: "An African-American woman in New Orleans was admitted into the hospital for a pregnancy termination. Two weeks later she received a check for $5,000. She phoned the hospital to ask who it was from. The hospital said, 'Crime stoppers.'"
5. June 2011: An e-mail described a man seeking to obtain "welfare" for his dogs because they are "mixed in color, unemployed, lazy, can't speak English and have no frigging clue who their Daddies are."
6. October 2011: An e-mail included a photo of a group of bare-chested women dancing, seemingly in Africa, with the caption, "Michelle Obama's High School Reunion."
7. December 2011: An e-mail included jokes that are based on offensive stereotypes about Muslims.

The report also showed a glaring disparity between the number of Black citizens stopped and arrested by police versus that of White citizens. Despite this deep scrape against the flesh of racial equality, its exposure and the vigil kept on racial profiling prove that America is changing its complexion. It is no longer Black versus White. We are now exploring the gray areas in which we meet and share the same principles and morals. America is a nation that is touched by the Hand of God; in many ways sanitized by the blood, sweat and tears of ancestral courage. The dignity with which our leaders from the past carried the burdens of societal injustice is more than commendable. The torch that we must all bear as spiritual beings compels us to reach past the color differentiation and inside the eyes of the Lord to see the brothers and sisters God intended us to be.

From Bliss to Betrayal

A season of bliss
A spiritual bond
Begins with a kiss
Ends in a sad song

"Love does not delight in evil but rejoices with the truth."

(1 Corinthians 13:6)

CHAPTER ELEVEN

From Bliss to Betrayal

We tend to believe that our feelings originate from our hearts; however, the poison that erupts from an infirmed mind can pierce the heart and drain the spirit. Feelings become a force that rages from the depths of a blighted soul, rather than the simple purity of warm internal bliss. It is this bliss that Jesus brought with Him when He came to earth. It is like the song of a lark, versus the ear-wrenching noise of the vulture. The lark has always been associated with Christ and His image as "the bread of life." This bird is known as the protector of the wheat, and because it nests on the ground, it is considered in biblical terms to symbolize the unity and protection of heaven and earth. The song of the lark is melodious, often causing other creatures to pause at the sound of its singing. British folklore promotes eating three lark eggs to obtain a beautiful singing voice. Like the lark, the Lord hums peace into our spirits, while a cacophony of sounds from the nest of the enemy deafens us to the call for love.

Louise Mason was a struggling businesswoman who found the love of her life strictly by accident during one of Beamont Martin's athletic events. He appeared to be strong, well-built, handsome, intelligent, and somewhat enigmatic. These were appealing traits to Louise; seductively so. Their courtship was filled with flowers, flattery, and at times, flamboyance as the dynamic suitor wooed her into believing their relationship was beyond reproach. Louise's spirit soared when her suitor asked for her hand in marriage.

Although he was known as a "ladies' man" for all the obvious reasons, Louise was drawn into his hypnotic web like an empty heart to a proliferation of love.

Through the years, their union produced three beautiful, talented, and caring young girls. Like their mother, their belief system rested on answering the needs of those who were bitten by the serpent of poverty, misfortune, and inner turmoil. Their father's role of provider, head of the family, and the traditional figure of omniscience was solid and palpable. The couple settled into a play with the actors all playing their roles admirably, in an old-fashioned family pattern with all the expectations being met without question. Louise loved Beau, as she lovingly referred to him, and she could feel his reciprocation from his touch and his contributions to the lives they created together. She managed to matriculate in one of the best universities in the country, becoming a well sought-after advisor in her field of higher learning. Beau supported her dreams and goals. Each lovely day seemed to bleed into the next without incident, except for the occasional minor disagreements regarding trivial matters like restaurant dining preferences.

It was a typical day in the Mason household. Beau kissed his wife gently and went to work as he had every other workday. He generally left work between 5:00pm and 6:00pm, arriving home no later than 6:30pm. Louise went through her daily activities, arriving home at 5:30pm. Her neighbor greeted her at the door, asking "Where do you get all of your energy? I noticed you and Beau riding around the community on that roaring motorcycle." Louise was incredulous. She explained to her neighbor that she was just arriving home, and neither she nor her husband owned or operated a motor bike. Her neighbor insisted that she saw Beau with a woman whom she thought was Louise on a motor bike, not only cruising from block to block, but entering and exiting Louise's home. The story was too unbelievable for Louise to mentally consume, so she invited her neighbor inside while she perused papers and paraphernalia in the house for evidence of her husband's presence.

The neighbor was in tow when she spotted two glasses near the sink in the kitchen. The glasses appeared to contain wine, so Louise examined the bottle the couple kept for special occasions in the refrigerator. It was half empty, to her amazement. She also noticed an ink pen Beau carried tossed across the kitchen table.

"Is there something wrong?" the neighbor asked alarmingly. Louise flopped on a kitchen chair and stared out the window in a trance like state. The ink pen provided the catalyst for her imagination, filtered by the reality of her neighbor's witness. Suddenly, she could feel the stir of emotions in the air. She could sniff the putrid odor of infidelity. Louise, mesmerized by what appeared to be the proverbial signs of an affair, carefully dismissed the presumptive inquisition of her neighbor. "I think I know what happened," she said smiling warmly. "We'll talk later." Louise led her nosy neighbor to the door, closing it quietly while a strong mask of dismay washed over her face. She sat silently in her living room chair waiting for Beau to return home. Calling was not an option because she needed to compose her thoughts.

She watched the pendulum rock in a synchronistic rhythm on the huge grandfather clock that was cradled in the corner of the room. Louise whispered, "Jesus, Jesus," softly with each movement. As tears collided against the powder on her face, she tried to remember the bible verses from her youth. 'The Lord is my shepherd. I shall not want.' The first verse of the twenty third psalm was all she could think about as she stared at the door, wondering what words would find their way off her tongue when Beau arrived. It was a painful wait. She reminisced about various joyful scenes in their marriage. The clock's hourly chime brought a jolt that sent electricity into her body. The clock would chime throughout the night while Louise kept vigilance on the wooden structure in front of her. It was an exercise in futility.

Love can be both liberating and incarcerating simultaneously. It frees the heart and the mind for trust and an all-encompassing euphoria that seduces the spirit into a sense of eternal ecstasy. Sometimes, particularly with the constant pacing back and forth from the fowler, love can be a chain that binds the emotions, terrifies the mind, and compromises integrity. Millions of women and even some men across the globe have found themselves staring at doors, emitting tears of woe, calling on the Lord, or cursing the day they met the person whom they once called the "love" of their lives. During these bouts of pain and regret, it is easy to take inventory of weight, age, personality, and attractiveness. Trying to understand what went wrong can override what went right between two people. The longest day in a relationship is the day that it finally hits a heart that the affection and respect that served as a bond in the relationship has morphed into a carnal mirage that separates and maligns. People cheat on their spouses. Cheating has existed since biblical times, and the painful sting leaves indelible scars on the spirit. Real love, however, is not based on the flesh. It is based on the transformation and uniting of two spirits blending into one. However, many couples ultimately find, "The spirit is willing, but the flesh is weak." (Matthew 26:41). "...the desires of the flesh and the desires of the eyes and pride in possessions—is not from the Father but is from the world. And the world is passing away along with its desires..." (I John 2:16).

Louise had more than twelve hours to relive comments made by her neighbor, evaluate a half empty wine bottle, and conduct a mental investigation into reasons why Beau spent the night away from home sans a phone call for explanation. She realized that she had her on explaining to do to her children, including why she had not been to bed, and where their father slept that night. These were not easy questions to answer under the circumstances, but she recognized her obligation to try. She raced to the bathroom to shower, and then quickly prepared a huge breakfast for the children. While they ate, and she drank her morning brew, she told them that their father was working on a special project and would probably not be home for a few days. She believed this would cover her confrontation, and his time spent away from the home thereafter. There was absolutely no way their "discussion" would end with Beau remaining in their home, at least not for a few days. She could feel the emotional abandonment rising through every nerve in her body as she stared at the door awaiting the moment of truth.

She agonized over the questions she would ask, and the responses he would give. Even while she prayed, she knew her life was drastically changed. Most wives know when their spouses have disconnected from their vows. It is as if the extra sensory perception that causes a mother to call a child when it is in trouble is deeply embedded in the union with a spouse. Infidelity rises from the shadows of lies and excuses, carrying with it an intolerable disregard for trust and commitment. The lack of sleep, coupled with the humiliation of knowing that her neighbor witnessed Beau's blatant disrespect for Louise, their children, and their family caused her to weep uncontrollably. Even while her sight was dulled by the steady stream of water filling her eyes, Louise cried to the Lord to help her understand, and conquer her plummeting spiritual melancholy. When

Beau did not come home, she decided to call him on his cell phone out of fear for his health and safety.

"Hey," he answered abruptly.

"Where are you and what's going on?" Louise responded trying to sound as calm as possible.

"Ah, we need to talk." Beau tripped over his words and Louise could hear the whisper of a woman's voice in the background.

"What do you mean, we need to talk? Did you bring another woman into the home that we share with our children?"

"That's what we need to talk about. I didn't mean to hurt you and the kids. I just fell in love." He continued awkwardly.

"Are you saying you want to leave me and the kids for her?" Despite her attempts at keeping the conversation as sedate as possible, Louise found her volume stirring in her voice.

"I'll be fair in the divorce settlement. You can have the house for the kids. I just want to be with my lady and live together in peace."

It is a common scene in many homes, particularly when a man reaches middle-age and begins calculating the number of years that may be left in his life. Louise was heart-broken, but she separated and divorced from Beau. It only took two years before he returned to their home asking Louise for another chance to make things right. Louise refused. It was not out of spite, hurt, or degradation; but an understanding that two people must be equally yoked for a relationship, a marriage, dating situation, even a friendship to last. "[But] whoso committeth adultery with a woman lacketh understanding he [that] doeth it destroyeth his own soul." (Proverbs 6:32). Beau became remorseful about the quick decision he made to toss away years of a solid union for moments of ill-gotten temporary pleasure. He did not realize until it was too late how much the wrong decision could and would cost him. He had not put his new lover to the tests that come with uniting in a bond of one or vowing to be there for one another for better or worse. When the worse came upon him and he had to look for work after losing his job and his money began draining from bills and paying support to the family he deserted, his lover quickly exited his life.

Couples should be more than partners; they should be best friends. Beyond the friendship, there should be some human decency that relegates admiration for beauty and seduction to the person with whom vows were taken and promises were made. The one thing we must all remember is that in the end, we will all look alike- regardless of race, color, gender, attractiveness, or unattractiveness. Our bodies will all go back to the dust from which we came, or the ashes the fires that consume our earthly shell. The most important part of any relationship has more to do with how much we value the endless beauty of that is shared by words born from harmonious spiritual intimacy, or the temporary attraction that debilitates with the first age line, waist expansion, and noise of muted monologues.

Unrequited Pain

Pure little child, drenched in tears
Dark tides from shores enrich your fears
A spirit smothered with tainted stain
Smeared on your journey of unrequited pain.

"Verily I say unto you, insomuch as you have done it unto these,
one of the least of my brethren, you have done it unto me"

(Matthew 25:40)

CHAPTER TWELVE

Unrequited Pain

A six-year-old girl walked hurriedly in the brisk wind on a sunny September day. It was 1957, and her gait matched her personality; joyful, youthful, and precocious. School had just started, and this child was basking in the innocence of playful frivolity as she trotted along with her new friends from her first-grade class. The era dictated a foot stepping type of transportation, and a certain joy that comes with not knowing the troubles of the world. She was heading to her after school spot, the home of family friends whom her parents were paying to keep her until they picked her up. It was her safety haven where she joined with other children in outdoor games until her parents' arrival after work.

She always loved the colors of autumn, the rich golden hues of leaves that succumb to the gusting winds of the season. Games like tag, hide-and-seek, and many others the children created during their outdoor adventures made these few hours precious to the child. The family friends, an older couple, the Harris' were like grandparents to the young girl. The grandmother figure had a peanut butter and jelly sandwich for her when she arrived. The grandfather figure usually sat on the porch in a traditional rocking chair smiling at the girl and the other children who frolicked on the Harris' huge front lawn.

The young girl laughed heartily as her friends attempted to touch her in a fierce game of dodge ball. She heard a voice in the distance calling her name, but she was enjoying the game too much to respond. The voice yelled louder, "Come here!" The child turned to see Mr. Harris sitting in his usual spot with his glass in his hand, sipping the contents and smacking his lips as if to reveal how refreshing the drink was. At that time, and during that era, children were taught to obey adults. This was learned behavior even before learning your A, B, C's, and just as important in most households. Respect for your elders was of great consequence, especially in homes where Christian beliefs and principles were the cornerstone of the family's belief system. The neighbors could scrutinize report cards, or respond to naughty behavior with corporal punishment, if they deemed it necessary. Being indoctrinated by this concept throughout her six years, the young girl knew even though her childhood interaction was bringing her joy, the fear of disobedience to an older caregiver held a stronger bond to her spirit. It also had a resonance to future tears from potential pain that could come to her back side.

Slowly, the young child moved toward the voice and the porch where Mr. Harris was now standing. As she got closer, he opened the house door. It was reminiscent of her father when he was disturbed by her actions. It was generally followed by "Get in this house...NOW!" Mr. Harris was not speaking in that tone; in fact, he seemed quite calm yet determined. When she reached the door, she began to smell a foul unidentifiable odor. He led her to the first room on the right, which had a high post bed, a dresser, and a lengthy mirror. 'I have no idea what I did, but I think I am going to get a whopping.' The child thought as she reluctantly stood at the threshold of the bedroom. Mr. Harris closed the door, and immediately unbuckled his belt. The girl closed her eyes and turned her face from him because she was certain one end of that belt would contact some part of her body, but she did not know her offense.

Harris' pants dropped to his knees, which would ordinarily make the silly child laugh, but there was something ominous and eerie about his facial expression. He walked over to the girl and put his hands where no man should, which horrified the child beyond words. His wife apparently noticed the closed bedroom door and missed the child's presence outside with the other youngsters. "Harris...Harris, where are you?" she asked in a somewhat shaky voice. Harris continued his molestation, and then quickly pulled up his pants. He reached inside his pants pocket, handed the young girl a quarter, then put his finger to his lips and whispered, "Shhhh." When he finally opened the door, his wife was standing on the other side. She looked at the disheveled girl, straightened out the hem of the child's dress, then sent her back outside to play with the other children. Somehow, the child no longer had an interest in playing with her peers. Something had drastically changed, and she could feel it in her mind, body, and spirit. It was so palpable, that a complete metamorphosis began in the child. She felt shame, guilt, and violated. It would be years before she could tolerate even an accidental brush against her skin from any man. The years also helped her to identify the strange smell that came from her attacker. It was the putrid foul odor of alcohol, an unfamiliar fragrance in her home.

There were at least five other little girls in the Harris' yard that day. They were all, in her mind, prettier, livelier, more attractive than she, but this man looked past all of them and selected her as his victim. It was not that she believed any of her playmates should endure the same lifetime lifelong torment that she experienced, but in her little girl mind, it was something that she did that caused her attacker to select her to assail. This idea would follow her throughout her life. This assault set the stage for the invisible cloud she often imagined hovering over her head, and the rejections she felt from trusted friends. Then there was a revelation. She was unable to trust any man who was not her father or brother, but through the test of time, and renewal of her spirit, she was able to dissect the incident spiritually.

It took twenty-three years for the child to divulge her secret to her parents. Mr. Harris had passed, and her parents lamented his departure from the earth, still believing him to be a great guy and a wonderful caretaker of her their child. Both parents remained silent as she told them few details but gave them the bottom line on how this grandfather figure became a nightmare source in her life. She could sense the great remorse emanating from both parents for what they realized was a violation of trust.

When someone becomes a source of evil intent, particularly through the purity of a child's spirit, there are scars that are embellished by the early episode. Additionally, when a child has learned the power of a Supreme Being who watches over her, there will be questions regarding the presence of God when a despicable act was perpetrated against her. Through the years, as the child matured into her teenage years, young adult phase, and ultimately middle age, she was able to decipher some reasons behind her experience. She deduced that her mission was to help people; those who offend and those who fall victim to offenders. She discovered a charisma that allowed many people to discuss with her their most confidential secrets and problems. It was amazing how people would pass through a crowd of friends and associates to bend the ear of this stranger with whom they felt a spiritual camaraderie. Her suffering produced sympathy and an empathy she probably would not have ordinarily have. That is the way with many people who have walked through the torrid terrors of life. There is generally a transformation, and a surge of confidence that God can bring you through any tragedy.

Although the fowler used his influence to corrupt the mind of Mr. Harris by introducing the overindulgence of a malevolent elixir that frayed his conscience and mutilated his spirit, his spiritual homicide against the child produced a change in heart for hundreds of people. Some she counseled found a closer alliance with God, and she was able to lead others through to a rejection of spiritual suicide in an attempt to understand their true-life purpose.

When the Apostle Paul was imprisoned and awaiting his appeal from Caesar, he boldly made statements about his faith in the Lord that changed the minds and hearts of his inmates, and those who experienced his courage. He declared "All things work together for good for those who love the Lord and are called according to His purposes." (Romans 8:28). God can use even the most devastating trials of our lives to create a renewed awareness of His eternal light that shines beyond this world. Even when the fowler instructs his followers to "kill, steal, and destroy," there is an aura from heaven that shines so brilliantly that the darkness of the fowler is engulfed by it. His wicked deeds and spiritual homicide become the enlightened path for our life's purpose and our spiritual resurrection.

Winter in a Summer Heart

Oh, chilling breeze beneath my soul
A season once entrenched in gold
Succumbs to lessons when spirits part
Bringing winter inside a summer heart.

"Bless them that curse you and pray for them which despitefully use you."

Luke 6:28

CHAPTER THIRTEEN

Winter in a Summer Heart

Time has proven that life contains moments that challenge our humanity and can sever the collective umbilical cord that we share with all of God's creatures. We never know where a day, an hour, or a minute can take us emotionally, nor can we determine how the consistency of challenge can affect our attitudes. The number of people who are willing to sacrifice for their fellow man is rapidly decreasing. It is a part of the inevitability that has been foretold by the bible about stony hearts and the evolution of the colder nature of mankind. It can also be attributed to reactions from negative events that unfold while we attempt to do God's will.

Some people are born with summer hearts; the warmth and sensitivity for the oppressed, the abused, and the victims of outrageous fates and fortunes that seem unimaginable. These are the people who place themselves in harm's way to stop a fight, to help an injured person, to rescue animals and people from burning houses, or to change the course of history through enormous sacrifice.

The rescuers during the 911 American tragedies whose lives were ended as they struggled to save lives all had summer hearts. It is not duty that drives them during a tragic event; it is an unseen force that has programmed their spirits to immediately react without fear of danger to save others. Men like Dr. Martin Luther King's, Jr. and James Meredith, who says he was on "A Mission from God" when he defied the prejudices of his time in 1962 to integrate Ole Miss, a glowing icon of bigotry for Mississippians and blacks throughout the nation during that era. James Meredith faced taunting, death threats, and when he prepared for his "Walk against Fear" he faced nearly fatal wounds because he always stepped to the beat of a celestial drummer. Today, his wife, Dr. Judy Alsobrooks Meredith says her husband is concerned about Christians evoking rights that reach beyond the prejudices aimed at Blacks from yesteryear. "James feels that institutions like Ole Miss, along with racist whites, are not the problem. We as Christians must learn to take care of ourselves." She says emphatically.

Quite often, summer hearts that blaze so brightly from the rays of heavenly light are eclipsed by the dark fog of spewing contempt. Constant battles from soldiers of the night entrapped by the chains of the fowler can change a summer heart into a winter wonderland. Those for whom the valiant fight can quickly become the enemy or create a situation that defies their "mission from God."

Humanitarians are often the target of vengeance because the fowler presents envy and jealousy as weapons against their generosity and kindness. After all, love of God is really the first of all commandments and loving our neighbor as we love ourselves is the second. We must remember that "we wrestle not with flesh and blood, but against principalities, against powers, against rulers of the darkness of this world, against spiritual wickedness in high places." (Ephesians 6:12). That battle between good and evil is the reoccurring theme in our lives; in fact, it is the cause of all the snares we encounter as we continue our journey in this world. Perhaps, the battle is tougher for God's human angels who must rise to all occasions for the sake of the occupants of this world while preparing for their cross over to the world beyond. God gave us mothers to help us understand the purity of love, sacrifice, and the enormous blaze that rages inside a summer heart.

Tamara Lewis was a single mother who raised her eighteen-year-old son in accordance with biblical beliefs. Marcus, like many young people, experimented with forbidden fruit, like smoking and imbibing alcohol; however, he was the epitome of the spiritually trained child Tamara taught. Marcus was a good college scholar who matriculated at a university that produced skillful medical students, many of which became noted physicians and nurses. Like any other youth, Marcus could endeavor in the pleasures of dating, dancing, and dallying about in the dark hours of the night. Student night clubs, parties, and all the glitz and glamour of seductive night life mesmerized Marcus, just has it has many before him, and will for many after him.

It was a clear night with a full moon glowing in full radiance when Marcus and his best friend Paul drove from party to party, meeting, and greeting fellow students who were experiencing the same rite of passage that comes in the spring of life. Beads of sweat popped on the faces of the students as they swayed and contorted their bodies rhythmically to the fast-paced bass that carried each tune. Then, it was off to the next adventure, and so it would go past the bewitching hour, and into the inaudible ticking of fate and misfortune. Suddenly, as the two laughing figures motored down a familiar street, the sound of sirens broke their levity and introduced Marcus and the unsuspecting Tamara to an incredible maze of legal and baffling tomfoolery. Marcus was arrested for the bizarre crime of robbing a drug dealer at gun point. There was no evidence, no witnesses, no rhyme or reason for his incarceration, or the years of anguish he and his mother spent in defending him against charges from this mysterious admitted criminal, yet he was a constant presence in courtrooms. After this bogus arrest, there were many others from assault to drug possession. Marcus is an articulate African American college student who is a black youth living in a part of the country that is not yet color blind. His greatest offense, like that of many other young black males, is going against a stereotype and moving toward the pursuit of the happiness that was presumably afforded to all by the Constitution of the United States. Tamara, like many other Christian mothers, faced the heartache of holding her distraught son together with one hand, and clenching tightly to the words of the Lord with an upraised fist in the other.

Each false charge chipped away at her reserve to keep her faith firm, which was knowing the goal of the enemy is to challenge her faith walk. The enemy has a specific tool and plan for every person he wants to consume. Consumption comes from loss of faith, disillusionment, fear, anxiety, and the notion that the evil thrust upon us by repetitive feats of despair will haunt us through perpetuity. When there is no rhyme or reason in this world for excessive hurt and pain, we must "Look to the hills from whence cometh our help. Our help cometh from the Lord who made heaven and earth." (Psalm 121:1-2). Yet, our minds dwell in a cavernous tomb when we are attacked by the enemy. It would be a few years before Marcus could break free from the anguish of legal forces that were aimed at him because of the limited years of his life, and the darkened hue of his skin. He and Tamara became vulnerable, gravitating toward the vacillation between the celestial light and dark side of each situation. It is the intoxication of the flesh battling against the sobriety of the spirit. This occurs often when we face temptations.

There is no cure for the common cold, or the ubiquity of its emotional counterpart, vulnerability. Symptoms of a cold are quite evident; however, those of vulnerability certainly go unnoticed by the common man. Its victims tend to love too hard, hurt too deeply, and reflect too often on what could have been. It is analogous to an open wound that oozes internal pain that only an enlighten spirit can diagnose, and a darken spirit can use for its own gratuitous greed. Many have suffered from both ailments and have concluded that a cold will eventually run its course; however, vulnerability can be eternal.

Vulnerability leads to errors in judgment that eclipse protective wisdom and fortify pretentious pleasure. Vulnerability is tantamount to constantly expecting something from acts that amount to the ultimate nothing, embarrassment and regret. Unless you have walked the path of Marcus and Tamara, you may not understand their perils; however, everyone at some time or the other has faced false accusation. Getting caught up in Satan's schemes requires many prayerful moments, in a moment of unbridled physical a release of what is carnal, and an increase in what is spiritual, for example, can mean a compromise of values and morality that leads to complications in the spiritual realm.

""Keep watching and praying that you may not enter into temptation..." Matthew 26:41

Often, we put ourselves in situations where temptation overrides the substance of our being. Our being is loftier than fornication and more tenacious than fear of lost desire.

"There is no fear in love; but perfect love casts out fear, because fear involves punishment, and the one who fears is not perfected in love." I John 4:18

Lust is often mistaken for love, and love can only be tested by measuring it through its biblical definition.

"Love is patient, love is kind, and is not jealous; love does not brag and is not arrogant, does not act unbecomingly; it does not seek its own, is not provoked, does not consider a wrong suffered, does not rejoice in unrighteousness, but rejoices with the truth; bears all things, believes all things, hopes all things, endures all things. Love never fails…"

Mary J. believed she was in love. Her beau was handsome, kind, generous, and appeared to be completely devoted to her. It was the 1970's when the Viet Nam War was raging, and young men were drafted. Many had a limited life expectancy, and couples grew closer because of their predictions of what might happen after they parted. Had they embraced for the final time, or expressed themselves through the warmth of pressed lips in some stunning last act of a Shakespearean type remorseful scene? Mary J. held her virtue in high esteem. Although each kiss with her beloved RJ sent spiraling sensations through her nerve within her, she was a Christian young lady who believed in saving her virtue for the blessing of matrimony. Although RJ tempted that virtue on a regular basis, Mary understood these temptations to be pedestrian by comparison to her faith walk with God.

RJ was drafted into the army during their college years. It was a devastating time in Mary's life. She could not begin to understand what might happen to her beloved boyfriend, the first relationship she ever had. After a multitude of kisses, and a very passionate night censored by Mary's virtue, RJ left school for the unpredictable fate of human forces. Since he was stationed at a nearby camp during his first months of boot camp, he often visited her; even going AWOL (absent without leave) to be with her. One day when RJ visited, a photo dropped from his sun visor while they were riding in his car. Initially, Mary J thought it is a picture of her, since the young lady's hair resembled her style. After more scrutiny, she discovered it was someone else. Many thoughts raced through Mary's mind, particularly when she noticed the young woman was dressed in army attire, but RJ said the young woman was just a friend. It was what Mary J trained her mind to believe. "Surely, he would let me know if he decided to date someone else. We have been so close, and I care so much for him," she thought as she took one last glance at the picture of the pretty private with the glowing teeth and petite facial structure before RJ grabbed it and carelessly tossed it in his wallet.

After that visit, it was a while before RJ called. His conversations were shorter and shorter. Finally, he called and said "Hello…Mary…" Then, she heard a woman chuckling in the background. RJ began laughing, too!

Suddenly there appeared to be a struggle with the phone. There was the dull sinister sound of a dial tone. She held the phone for a few minutes, hearing a cacophony of increasing thumps in her chest, and the endless refrain of that menacing electronic hum in her ear. Her body was paralyzed like a suctioning of spirit exiting every corridor of her being. It would be a few months before she heard that RJ and his giggling companion were married.

It took years for Mary J to comprehend the boundaries of her relationship. She often pondered over her decision about chastity, as she traced every step of what she believed to be a true bond that did not require the worldly physical acts of unmarried horizontal motions. Through the years, Mary J grew aloof, particularly in her relationships with men. She was robotic in her dating life and had no desire to seek any lasting commitments with her male acquaintances. A young woman filled with a loving heart, noble intentions, and the zest for a soul mate, had become an unfeeling caretaker of a heart that slowly split on that one momentous summer day when RJ treated their relationship like a joke of which she was the punch line.

It is a natural response to blame ourselves, our actions, even our lack of action when relationships fizzle from dreams of the future to stories of the past. What we desire is not always what God sees as best for us, and He has a panoramic view of what lies ahead. Some things like so called "lost relationships" are blessings that defy our ability to understand the plan for our lives. Through the pain of loss, our strength is multiplied, our full armor of God is built, and our wisdom blossoms. "Experience is the best teacher, IF you can SURVIVE the experience," my father, James Edward Flanders, Sr. often said. Once you survive the experience, you can thrive and really enjoy being alive, because you begin to acknowledge in your spirit that life is not a fairy tale, and there is no "happily ever after" until we cross from this plane into the eternal one that our heavenly Father promises on the other side of this dimension. Just like seasons, we are always changing because of our experiences, both joyful and sad. Sometimes, a summer heart, filled with a plethora of emotions, and a hunger for giving and receiving love must endure a winter where dreams are frozen, and the flowers of our youth yield to the passing winds of time.

By Journey's End

Hush, and feel the cry of your soul
A spiritual whisper, the body's parole
The stilling of clocks once pounding in youth
The final tick-tock of yesterday's truth
Do stare at the moon and run through the rain
Feel the vanishing presence of loss and gain
Forgive me, dear Lord while I inwardly weep
For your words of wisdom awaken my sleep.

*"Behold, I shew you a mystery; we shall not all
sleep, but we shall all be changed…"*

I Corinthians 15:51

CHAPTER FOURTEEN

By Journey's End

Hattie "Shotgun" Davis was a walking contradiction to family and friends. Although she was extremely kind and loyal, her temper could catapult anyone who crossed her path into another world, literally. "She was known in the neighborhood as 'Shotgun Hattie' because when she was tired of hearing a police helicopter buzzing around in the sky, she took her shot gun and shot it out of the sky. "True story," says her niece who remained close to Davis throughout her life. The incident was reported in area newspapers during the 1970's, which solidified Hattie's "reign of terror" throughout the neighborhood and with area law enforcement. Shotgun earned her moniker even beyond the antics of this anecdote passed from generation to generation throughout her poverty infested neighborhood. during the 1970's. "My aunt stood about six feet one inch tall. She was once arrested for walking down the street naked with only a large python snake draped around her body," her niece reminisces. This tall brown toned blue-eyed beauty was known for more than the terror she brought to onlookers. She also earned a reputation for generosity, caring, and humor. She was known to literally give the shoes off her feet if she believed someone needed them. The contradiction between the two personalities often baffled relatives, friends, and those who gazed upon Hattie with both fear and reverence.

"Nobody messed with my aunt, especially the people she dated, because they realized that she could be dangerous when she became angry, but anyone could come to her with a money problem, or if they needed food and shelter, and she would find a way to provide them with what they needed."

According to her niece, her anger was triggered quickly, and her punishments were instantaneous and insufferable. Although she walked on both sides of the sexual fence, she appeared to favor men, most of whom knew her reputation. Some of her suitors feared her, but secretly challenged her in some "love of bad girls" type of attraction. There were many men of various characters who waltzed in and out of Hattie's life, but their exit had to be on her terms. That was one known condition of dating the infamous "Shotgun Hattie," and those who pursued her understood unfaithfulness could be dangerous or fatal. Paul apparently realized this Achilles heel that lied openly in the character of his lover, but his inebriated state altered his perspective, and ultimately his life.

November 10, 1975 was a relatively cold day in the south, but that did not curtail the partying and fish fries in the lower income communities. It was one of the few pleasures enjoyed by those who often lived without heat, or the proper raiment to fit the impending blistering elements of winter. After hour drinking holes, often called "honky tonks" were as plentiful throughout the city as restaurants. There were only a few that had regular patrons and just like the historic TV series, "Cheers," everybody knew their names; however, they were not always glad they came. Sometimes, these hidden "holes in the wall" were fraught with fist fights, stabbings, arguments, and all from the juiced-up drinkers who were more than willing to pay nearly half of what they would pay in a more legitimate establishment. These were generally small empty houses that could hold about twenty people, but more than fifty or sixty managed to squeeze into the quasi- cozy space. Most of these patrons made room by sitting on each other's laps. Loud music, billowing smoke, screeching voices, and red eyed soldiers of misfortune provided the ingredients for potential calamity and chaos. That often occurred on weekends when hard-working men and women decided to tie one on to escape their grueling existence in what was then called "shot gun houses." The name referred to rectangular houses in which the front and back doors were aligned so that if both were open, you could see straight through to the other side, with only twelve feet or less in between. They contain only three to four rooms and no hallway. Built after the civil war to allow those of meager means to have a domicile, there are still many in existence, primarily in the southern states. Strangely enough, most of the drinking holes were also shot gun houses, designed to create the illusion of an imaginary romantic oasis.

November was a peak time for drinking holes, particularly the popular ones. The upcoming holidays often brought euphoria and depression simultaneously to the denizens in the community. Drinking and swaying to a slow melodic song seemed a welcome pastime. Paul, like many other men in the community, relied on multiple partners for his romantic moments. Although he and Hattie appeared to be inseparable, there were still some ladies who could turn his head. It would be a costly neck roll when Paul snapped around to invite Peggy to a night of romance November 10th; one that would not be forgotten for years to come.

Peggy enjoyed the company of many suitors. She was a youthful forty whose personality and smile ignited a beauty of which many men had succumbed. Her reputation as a "good time girl" proceeded her, but it did not reach the level of promiscuity to those who craved even a moment of her prolific dating time. Paul watched Peggy from a distance initially. He studied her walk, the way she touched her hair while talking to men, and the slight swirl in her hips when she was courting attention from a potential partner. Hattie was working on this evening, and the timing to approach the seductive "Queen of Night," Peggy, seemed almost prophetic. Paul swaggered over to Peggy carrying a scotch and soda in one hand while extending the other in a polite request to dance. The music was soft and slow, an old tune that marked the mood of an alluring promise. Peggy and Paul swayed in rhythm with the high pitch of Minnie Riperton's "Loving You." The lyrics and sounds led from embrace to kiss, and soon the two were engaged in more intimate yet sedate dance floor movements. They were oblivious to the comings and goings of other patrons. No one noticed that Hattie was standing near the doorway glaring at the couple with scorn and surprise. It was an obvious affront to her seemingly cohesive bond with Paul, and it was embarrassing because everyone in the after-hour's handout hangout was aware of her relationship with Paul. Hattie approached the pair with fire in her eyes and devastation in her heart, a fatal combination for a combustible personality. Paul spotted her first and tore his hand from Peggy's waist immediately. He was aware there was more than a little trouble brewing from this legend of disruptive temperament.

Hattie sprang into action with squeals of discontent reaching volumes that threatened the ear drums of the others in the room. She grabbed Paul and put her hands around his neck while Peggy jolted for the door.

Someone in the room tried to subdue Hattie, realizing there was clear danger in the air, not only for Hattie's scorned infidel, but perhaps for every person in her path. This interruption gave Paul and Peggy enough time to escape from Hattie's grasp and scurry out into the darkness of uncertainty beyond the forbidden doors of their illegal party palace. As they ran through the streets together, they had no idea that Hattie was close behind them; nor did they see the large iron pipe she was brandishing as she chased after them. Despite their speedy gait, Hattie managed to catch up with Paul just as Peggy fell to the ground. Clumsily attempting to get back to her feet, Peggy watched in awe as Hattie beat Paul to the ground with the iron pipe. She ran feverishly screaming for help and managed to get the attention of someone on the street. As Paul lay washed in a pool of liquid fury, Hattie disappeared while the man-on-the-street helped him to climb to an upright position. The remnants of his attackers' displeasure rained from his head in gushes of blood.

Stained and unbalanced, Paul headed for his omnipresent safety haven, his sister's apartment. When he arrived at the door, his sister, Gerri, was astonished. Paul was somewhat disoriented, but he remained in a conscious and lucid state; enough to explain how he received his injuries and why. She immediately rushed him to the hospital, where they quickly treated him then discharged him. The following day, Paul's sister took him back to the hospital, where he was diagnosed with a brain clot. He spent several weeks in a semi-comatose state vacillating between this world and eternity. Meanwhile, Hattie spent her time trying to justify her behavior. Although the police were called and she was charged with assault, she was released from jail. The price of her dignity seemed to outweigh the value of Paul's life.

Paul was ultimately released from the hospital, but seven months later, he died. According to his physicians, Paul died as result of the injuries he sustained after Hattie bludgeoned him with the iron pipe. It was then that Hattie was arrested for second degree murder, or of which she was tried and found guilty. As a testament to her innate humane spirit, police testified that she was basically a "good person who gave them no trouble."

Hattie had an impoverished background, filled with alcoholism, rape, and dysfunction. Her life was strewn with improprieties at which most people would cringe or maybe even regurgitate if they had to endure such pain. There were no constant religious reminders of a Higher Power that generates love and affection to His people. All she knew was the ungodly carnal pursuits of a world drenched in momentary self-gratification. Despite her heritage, she was acquainted with something that reached beyond her sphere of influence; something more celestial that nagged at her heart and gave her a conscience. She experienced great regret for her actions, even though the legal system was flawed in its assessment of her role in Paul's death. Since Paul died seven months after he was afflicted by the blows Hattie swung at his head, her attorney did not argue the fact that he may have injured himself after the original incident. Legally, it could have been argued that he died from another ailment or condition, but during the 1970's, particularly in the south, it was difficult at best to find a court appointed defense attorney who would delve into this kind of case beyond the measure of mere duty. It was the proverbial "black-on-black" crime that is often overlooked, but generally expected from the low-income participants who choose to become the stars in their own tragic drama.

Hattie sat stoically in the quiet courtroom while Paul's sister described the agony her brother felt because of his injuries, and how much effort she put into saving him. The quivering voice of a devastated relative conjured up sorrowful emotions that nullified any concepts of being a "jilted lover" or losing face with a community of devastated neighbors who once enjoyed moments of levity and laughter with the Hattie and Paul duo. What screamed through the silence was the notion that in one whimsical frenetic conclave of demonic session and possession, a mere memory remained where a heart, a movement, a kiss and a hug in the form of an individual was now permanently erased.

Hattie loved Paul, but she was trapped in a quandary of saving herself from years inside the frosty steel environment of a prison cell and admitting to a crime for which her heart was paying a severe price. Either way, the punishment for his death was extremely difficult for her to bare. She thought of her young son whom she birthed seven years prior. He was the prize of her existence; the rambunctious ball of energy that seized her spirit and transformed her moods. Who would provide shelter for this poor little boy who may not see his mother again until he had grown into manhood? Hattie's actions appeared to be senseless, but a driving force, usually alcohol induced, pummeled her into a personality of which she had little or no control. Alcohol stirred up a restless spirit inside her; one that was intolerant of perceived disrespect. It was an emotion left over from the days of playing parent to her ten brothers and sisters when her parents were carousing in the liquid splendor of inebriation. It was Hattie the youngsters turned to for survival skills when the cupboards were empty, and their stomachs were growling. It was Hattie, who found creative, if not legal, methods of providing what they needed while living in the trenches of despair and desperation. That kind of responsibility for a young girl can be all the fodder the fowler needs for invasion. Hattie had so many previous convictions of violence against other men, including most of her previous five husbands, that an obvious pattern of behavior had been established during the years she protected her younger sisters and brothers. She also had on file sixty-three convictions for public intoxication, along with many other infractions for which she was given a lenient sentence. Although she served as the guiding force in her youth for her siblings, unfortunately, she could not seem to find a reciprocal protector in her own life. She had not yet uncovered the shield that comes through the power in the word of God. The darkness of a lonely heart that has not been gardened with the seeds of faith often produces the fruit of disruption and resentment.

The trance-like state in which Hattie found herself was abruptly interrupted when her name was called to take the stand. Although she was repentant about Paul, her confidence did not wane when she walked to the stand with her head in the air. Composure was not her strongest suit, but her personality beamed with so much illumination, it was difficult for even the judge to take issue with her sarcasm.

(Prosecutor)	"Have you been convicted of another murder?
(Hattie, looking cocky)	"Yes, I have."
(Prosecutor)	"All right. Who did you murder?"
(Hattie)	"Michael Mullen."
(Prosecutor)	"When was that?"
(Hattie)	"That was when I was twenty-seven years old."
(Prosecutor)	How old are you now?"
(Hattie)	"I was fifty-two Monday."

(Prosecutor)	"Were you drunk at the time you murdered Michael Mullen?"
(Hattie)	"No, I just got off work. No"
(Prosecutor)	"...On the 28th of August 1974, you didn't throw lye on a person named John Fredericks?"
(Hattie)	"He broke in my house, and I threw lye on him, and he cut me. That's why I threw lye on him."
(Prosecutor)	"Are you sure there wasn't another time you threw lye on somebody?"
(Hattie)	"Say what? What did you say, now?" she asked stretching her eyes. "No, I threw it at my husband. My husband beat me one time, and other than that, no."

It was what Hattie knew in her life; defending herself against the abuses of a world that appeared to be her enemy. She seemed to be seeking situations that would validate the theme of her earlier years, the one that echoes through experience, 'there is no protection, love, or mercy for you. You must stay in a warlike state in order to survive.' Ultimately, Hattie would be sentenced to involuntary manslaughter and serve fifteen years in prison.

During her years of incarceration, she began to read the bible and pray profusely for forgiveness from a Higher Power. One day while still imprisoned, she received a call telling her that her beloved son was killed after he had threatened the life of a rival. The rival shot and killed him. In many ways, her son was her only connection to "good wheat;" the sprouting of something beyond the brutality and chaos she had known in her world. The sound of shackles bounced off church walls from the chains jeweled around Hattie's hands and feet. She walked slowly toward the dark brown casket that embedded her child while armed guards guiding guided her down the aisle. Her mind and heart cried out for God to "guard her heart" in the most distressing moments she could have ever faced. It was the hour of intense mourning of which only a mother who has lost her only child can understand. Hattie had reached her turning point years prior, but if indeed, her spiritual report card could appear, she would have received an "I," for her life's journey was incomplete.

After being released from prison, Hattie spent her time talking to neighbors, friends, and the needy strangers she boarded and fed about the power of God and His child, Jesus Christ. She insisted that those who once called her "Shotgun" with a wink in their voices, eliminate that word from her signature page. She was Hattie, a woman whose world revolved around doing as much good in the world as she could until the day she died. Her niece talks about what a wonderful person she became post incarceration. "She was the kindest, gentlest creature you could ever meet. She was the kind of person who could feel the pain of others and reacted to it immediately in a positive way." Hattie became weak, and soon discovered she had pancreatic cancer. She no longer had a concern with where she was going after leaving earth, but she was distressed by the pain the disease brought her. It was pain that only lasted a few months. When she died, those who knew her remembered the sweetness in her spirit, the joy she brought to others, and the message that she carried through actions, words, and deeds about the glory of God.

Although the fowler seduced Hattie for a while, the Maker of the fowler and the universe had bigger plans for her future on earth and in heaven. There is little doubt from those who knew her that she resides happily in the latter.

Dangerous Translations

Tears through memories ripped by tortuous pain
Intense dark spirits resurrected again
Beckoning the soul through a portal of escape
Leaving one final gesture at heaven's gate.

*"Yea, though I walk through the valley of the shadow of
death, I will fear no evil for thou art with me."*

Psalm 24:4

CHAPTER FIFTEEN

Dangerous Translations

The thought of taking your own life is like wading through the murky depths of dark waters, gulping on the toxins in a sea of despair. It is the most alone a person can feel without being lonely. The consumption of this wave of ebony tide is not a force that begs for company; nor does it breed the overture of sympathy. Voices that once rose harmoniously through the walls of your mind begin to resonate in accelerating discord. Suddenly, there is an empty silence and an enclave of scorners rallying around your debilitated spirit like an army of imps vying for your soul. A chill permeates your entire being ushering in scenes of the arrival and departure of love, laughter, joy, and peace that wash over your mind, then abandon you quickly as if they never existed. The cold midnight of the moment crawls inside of you making you a part of the nothingness never really seen or heard. The moment in which a decision is made to end your life is the time in which the fowler kidnaps your mind and screams inside your spirit, "You never really mattered." What an insult to our Creator!

The enemy understands our earthly mission and uses his power to overtake the purpose God has for us. According to the bible, ""Therefore submit to God. Resist the devil and he will flee from you." (James 4:7) Our struggle is not against flesh and blood, but against the rulers, against the powers, against the world forces of this darkness, against the spiritual forces of wickedness in the heavenly places." (Ephesians 6:12). According to the word, the devil is conceited, self-absorbed, vain and independent of the rules of the Lord, which is why he was cast from heaven. The act of ending your life is the ultimate form of vanity and self-absorption. It means you no longer believe that God, the Master Healer, the Director of Fate, can restore that which has been stolen from your life. The carnal world is set up by Satan, along with its power to beckon our fleshly senses and urges to the point of obsession.

There is something in each of us that triggers inexplicable joy and unbearable pain. Some of these triggers are common, like that blissful feeling about someone whose presence conjures an avalanche of emotional and physical response beyond control. Some call it "chemistry," others define it as a spiritual connection. Whatever the label, it changes our demeanor and alters our behavior when we think of a specific person, or activity. Pain has the same reaction in reverse. It can originate from words, actions, or spirits emanating from dark places; unfiltered and venomous. Every circumstance or scene in our lives paints broad strokes with soft or bristled brushes signaling contentment or chaos. Many scholars and psychologists suggest that our emotional contracts with people and situations develop as we script our roles around them based on our feelings about ourselves. Biblically, as we examine the stories about the relationships between Cain and Abel, Joseph and his brothers, we begin to learn that some scenarios occur beyond the frail constructs of human consciousness.

In his writing, "Happiness in this World," Dr. Alex Lickerman suggests there are six reasons why people attempt or complete suicide: "1) They are depressed 2) They are psychotic 3) The are impulsive 4) They are crying out for help 5) They have a psychological desire to die 6) They made a mistake." As a person who has taken this step into the deep side of malevolent suicidal ocean, I believe the fowler, Satan, understands your importance to God and manipulates your mind to destroy the mission God has set in motion for your life. It has always been my theory that before we are released into this nebulous planet called earth, we stand in certain lines in heaven. Some people line up to be givers in life, generating a momentum of spiritual generosity that is necessary for the fulfillment of God's words. "It is more blessed to give than to receive." (Acts 20:35). Factually, this scripture deals with assisting the weak; therefore, the generous with their hearts set in motion by heavenly things would be stronger than others. Others stand in the receivers' line. We must recognize for the Lord's words to take seed, grow, and blossom, there must be those with whom the givers share. Likewise, in my mind, there are lines for sensitive souls who embrace every human activity with a rush of spiritual adrenaline; savoring and collecting every emotion like method performers struggling to learn lines in a very long scripted play. Contrasting the delicate emotional actors are the lines filled with apathetic participants whose emotional walls appear impenetrable, yet they are also destined to be included on our life's unpredictable stage. There are also those who straddle many heavenly lines, darting in and out like character actors uncertain of when they should make their cameo appearances in our lives.

When characters are introduced and scenes begin to change, everyone is not prepared for the next act. Those of us who get lost because our roles morph into something unexpected, or we lose a protagonist, or discover that someone we believed to be a hero in our story is an antagonist, the scene calls for strength that eludes mere human faculties. Many of us decide to simply exit the stage. We tend to forget that we are not the director of our lives; God is. He is the playwright who decides how the story ends, and His storyline is a mystery to us. When He changes the scene, if we continue looking to Him for direction, we will see that He does so for the ultimate good of the player and the play. We get caught up in one act, maybe one that seems extended beyond the limits of our imagination, and the plot twist catapults our belief system into a spiral of depression. The camera lens in which we view our lives becomes cloudy with debris from mistakes, missed dreams, protagonists that suddenly become antagonists, misplaced allegiances and alliances, and a misunderstanding of our purpose on this planet. That is when faith comes into the play.

I was twenty-four years old, working in an industry of which I had dreamed, and being blessed in countless ways when I decided to end my life. A cacophony blending of odious declarations rising against me from "friends," betrayals and chameleons overwhelmed me. It was a time when my years of inexperience with the need for ubiquitous faith abandoned me. My spirit was assassinated by the empowerment of negative energy that attacked my sense of self. I was and am a child of the most High God, and whatever He allowed in my life was meant to teach me wisdom and strengthen me for the remaining acts and scenes of my existence. My adorable, patient, and spiritually enlightened mother was the instrument God used to save my life. My mother had a vision that I was dying, and called my then brother-in-law, insisting that he enter my apartment. The apartment manager reviewed what he had seen the night prior to my botched suicide attempt. I was sitting near the woods at the end of a cul de sac, pensively staring into the darkness of unpledged tomorrow's contemplating a permanent nap with the trees. Of course, there was no way this manager could know this; however, he drove slowly to where I sat and scorned me for being alone in a deserted part of the complex. I was coerced into returning to my apartment to complete my nearly fatal mission. As the hours drifted taking my breath with them, I had no recollection of the rescue efforts that were being made on my behalf. Years later when a few were willing to talk about the incident, I was told that my brother-in-law convinced the apartment manager to open my door, after countless attempts to get my attention by knocking feverishly. They found me on my couch in a fetal position very close to death. An ambulance was called, and I was pronounced dead. My brother-in-law would not accept it, so he pummeled me with his fists until the medics finally got a pulse. When I awakened in the hospital with tubes in every orifice of my body, I recall trying to tell the doctor not to tell my parents. I did not know at the time that my mother's view from God's eyes was the reason I was alive.

There was shame mixed with guilt that infiltrated my conscience. My father was in a veteran hospital at the time of my suicide attempt, in another part of the state. My mother was strained by the tension of driving miles from home to assist in his healing process and trying to protect me from myself. Suicide is a selfish act; one that I now recognize as an assurance to the fowler that his insidious malevolence was one method of stopping God's purposes and promises for my life. There are many who struggle down the path of adversity, armed with either enormous self-confidence or incredible self-doubt. Those with self-confidence have a propensity for overcoming a myriad of obstacles because they believe all things are possible. It is a form of faith that is lacking in those with self-doubt. It is my belief that even those who believe they are operating from their own sheer will are igniting and living under the principles of faith, as assessed by the bible, whether they credit God or any force beyond themselves. The spiritual definition of faith is "...The substance of things hoped for, the evidence of things not seen." (Hebrews 11:1). When faith is put into action, a positive energy is released in both the celestial and earthly realms. Many of those who thrive amid betrayals, false accusations, lies and deceit are navigating through the pit of perdition unwittingly wearing the crown of heaven. By contrast, the lack of faith produces depression, negativity, and the thought that nothing good can ever come out of a barrage of bad situations. Yet, many parables in the bible are designed to demonstrate how God uses some of the most iniquitous situations in the lives of His children to showcase the value, validity, and power of faith.

It has been said by many life observers, psychologists, law enforcers, and just plain folk who witnessed the many mazes of life that jealousy and envy are the most dangerous emotions, often carrying with them the forces of death. Satan is jealous of God, which is the reason that he is tenacious about enticing souls to join his army. He uses jealousy as a tool to manipulate the mind and encourage one person to wound another. Consider the story of the teenage boy, Joseph, who was despised by his brothers because of Jacob, their father's love for this youngest sibling. Already the set up for jealousy arises from a multi-colored coat made for young Joseph by his father. Joseph had ten older brothers, but not one of them looked upon the boy as someone whom they could also admire, protect, or simply love. They were so caught up in the fact that their father spent more time with this child, even though Joseph was born to an older man who believed his child production days had long since ended. They mocked Joseph, particularly when he revealed a dream that God stretched before him like a movie; one that would determine his fate and develop his faith. Joseph innocently revealed to his brothers a dream interpreted to mean that one day his brothers would bow before him. It was an incredulous notion to ten young men who looked upon the last in this line of boys with disdain simply because he was the last born. They planned to eliminate Joseph, so When his father sent Joseph to find his brothers in the far away fields where they were grazing their flock, the brothers saw him coming. The story of how they mocked him because of his dream resonates with many who have faith in a purpose that God whispers in a still small voice to all of us. It sometimes comes in a talent or skill, or it comes in a desire or wish. We each carry an innate dream that is as unique to us as a fingerprint. Instead of building their dreams, Joseph's brothers were adamant about erasing his, along with his life. Now in which they decided to throw him into an empty cistern to be devoured by animals, in a moment of slight compassion, Judah, one of the brothers decided it would be kinder to sell Joseph, collect some money, and relieve their consciences by having no blood on their hands for killing their brother. Ultimately, as the story goes, the brothers had to turn to Joseph when he was made king, and they bowed to him without recognizing the prey they once tossed in a ditch.

Joseph was betrayed greatly by the wife of his employer who falsely accused him of making unwanted advances, yet he was still destined to become king. The dream burned inside his heart and he realized no matter the appearance of things, God had a purpose beyond what was visible by mere human vision. So, it is with so many of us whose dreams become drenched in a pool of human interactions, rather than in the spiritual promises of our Heavenly Father. Our pain becomes our purpose when we can release it to God's holy intentions. The troubles I have endured since that fateful day when I tried to break my heavenly contract are far too great to share in one book, or even twenty. The day after my mother passed, my aunt succumbed to Alzheimer's disease and died. Eight months and one day after my mother died, my father joined them. Four months later, my uncle left this earth. Six months later, I was diagnosed with breast cancer. Seven surgeries and two major infections later, I am sharing my personal thoughts and those of other weary travelers for the sake of saving someone from the tyranny of misconceptions about this nebulous excursion called life.

Every time I see an octogenarian struggling for breath through a plastic tube, or an infant whose facial structure is distorted by its mother's drug addiction during pregnancy, or any person gripping a steel plated device to assist them in walking, I cringe at the ignorance of the acts that brought me to a semi-lifeless state. The infirmed, the impoverished, the abused, the taunted, the scorned, and the scorners are all connected by our disconnection of the celestial umbilical cord that once adjoined our need for being a part of a whole purpose. This temporary visit to a place that is not our real home confounds our minds and drives us into believing that the circumference of our world begins and ends with the inner sanctum we create. We suffer alone because the "me" in us has systematically crucified the "we" for which we were created. Satan's diabolical methods of separating us from each other just as his vanity separated him from heaven are intrinsic in our compassionless views of why some suffer more than others. Even Christians with biblical erudition often invoke their prejudices against their fellow man and offer scripture as a tool of reference.

Time can be a mocker with a mirror that reflects the distant past inside a limited future. The entrances and exits of those with whom we share our dreams can be swift, sudden, and shocking. Each time we say "good-bye" or "I love you" so casually at the end of a conversation could easily be the final words we utter or hear from someone we assume we will speak with again. Yet, we continue to treat each moment as a discarded trite release of another unappreciated breath, punctuated with a sigh that signals boredom. Facing and surviving breast cancer, attempted suicide, the loss of parents, family members, beloved friends, and the idea of mortality taught me that the life I was so quick to carelessly toss away has some value to God. Lyrics to Charlie Chaplain's composed song, "Smile" has great meaning for me, as it did for Michael Jackson. "Smile, though your heart is aching. Smile, even though it's breaking..." I have learned the joy of finding golden nuggets amid the garbage that is piled upon the spirit. I have even learned that every person who comes into your life, albeit for purposes of joy or pain has an important role that is necessary for growth.

I picture a scene on a stage in my mind during the culmination of my life. The voice of God announces each player, and every person who injured or helped me comes out to take a bow. "Playing the boisterous liar who falsely accused you of infractions you never even thought of is...." That real life character who caused me so much pain and angst will walk to center stage, smile and take a bow. I will be able to see how what they did changed the direction of my life and made me evaluate my own thoughts and deeds. Perhaps, they just happened to be in one of my imaginary heavenly lines for that reason. Maybe their purpose was as meaningful in my life as Joseph's brothers was in his. After all, if they had not sold him into slavery, all the other events in his life could not occur as they did. Before we condemn the haters, maybe we should rejoice at their condemnation because without it, we might never be able to define our presence and recognize our mission on earth. Even when the fowler uses his most loyal disciples, God's hand directs and limits their movements. As the adage goes, "The devil might have brought it, but God sent it."

When a dream adorned by faith gets caught in the fowler's snare, assassination is the ultimate goal. Only the belief in God's words and their strength can defy the source and resurrect the determination to continue down the path of His purpose. "We have escaped like a bird from the fowler's snare; the snare has been broken, and we have escaped." (Psalm 124:7).

SEVEN DAYS

OF STORIES AND PRAYERS
TO RESURRECT THE SPIRIT

MONDAY

There was once a child who was extremely afraid of what he had heard about the "boogeyman." At times when he was in his room alone and darkness covered his closet and bed, he felt uneasy about what might be lurking in the corners, under the bed, or in his closet. Instead of turning on the light, he decided the safest thing to do was to speak to the "boogeyman" and reason with him. "I love the boogeyman. I love the boogeyman." He thought his chant would endear the mythical creature to him, and no harm would come to him.

Like this innocent child, sometimes what we fear the most; depression, rejection, oppression, we begin to embrace unwittingly. In the midst of his troubles, Job said "For what I fear comes upon me, and what I dread befalls me. (Job 3:25). We can face the boogeyman, any man, any woman, or any situation knowing that God is the superhero in any story. He has already destroyed the boogeyman; all we must do is believe and have faith.

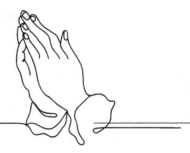

Dear God,

Today I walk by faith and not in fear. I choose to believe that whatever I face today, you are beside me, in front of me, and constantly around me to save me from all harm. In Jesus Christ name I pray, Amen. "The LORD is my light and my salvation– whom shall I fear? The LORD is the stronghold of my life– of whom shall I be afraid?" (Psalm 27:1)

TUESDAY

There is an old gospel hymn called "Bringing in the sheaves," that has been sung in churches throughout the country since it was written in 1874. Sheaves are bundles of plants that are often turned into cereals; wheat, corn, rye, and were gathered by workers during harvest season. The refrain of the song is: "Bringing in the sheaves…Bringing in the sheaves. We shall come rejoicing. Bringing in the sheaves."

Children and adults do not always hear the lyrics of a song correctly. One little boy during the 1930's sat next to his grandmother and sang in a high volume, hoping the spirit of the song would be evident in his small voice. "Bringing in the sheets…Bringing in the sheets…" He admitted in later years that he believed sheets were very holy items, until someone showed him the true lyrics of the song when he became an adult.

There are times when what we say does not match a situation, or it not what the person with whom we are speaking needs to hear. We do not understand the pain and anxieties that our words can add to circumstances, minds, and spirits.

"He that goeth forth and weepeth, bearing precious seed, shall doubtless come again with rejoicing, bringing his sheaves with him." (Psalm 126:6)

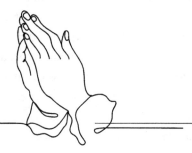

Dear Lord,

Please let my words reflect the kindness and consideration that you have for us. Let my mouth express healing and comfort so that I enhance the life of someone who needs to hear from you. In your holy and mighty name, I pray, Amen

WEDNESDAY

A woman was caught speeding down a busy highway in a congested city. Her mind was focused on the work she had to do that day, and she was running late for the office. When an officer pulled her over, he asked for her license and registration. "Ma'am, did you know you were going 85 miles per hour in a 65 mile per hour speed zone?" He was looking down grabbing for his pen to write the ticket when she said, "Officer, I am surprised. As fast as I was going, I was certain I was doing 90." The officer looked back at the woman's angelic face and gave her a smile. He had never encountered a person who seemed so genuinely honest; one who not only agreed she deserved a ticket but was willing to confess to a greater offense. "I am going to give you a warning today, but you must slow down." Shocked at her good fortune, the woman said, "Thank you, officer. You just made my day." She thought she had died and gone to Highway Heaven.

When we admit our wrongdoings, God is quick to forgive us. If we carry this tradition on in our daily lives, there would be fewer confrontations, disturbances, and arguments.

"If it is possible, as far as it depends on you, live at peace with everyone." (Romans 12:18)

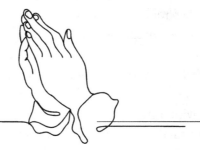

Dear Father,

If I offend anyone today, please give me the purity of heart to apologize. Let me keep a peaceful tongue and admit when I am wrong for the sake of harmony, and to release my soul and spirit from the confusion that comes with arrogance. In the name of Jesus Christ I pray, Amen.

THURSDAY

A woman went to the bank to withdraw funds from her account with hopes to enjoy a fun-filled day with a friend. When she got to the teller's window, the teller told her that her account was withdrawn by nearly $600. Upset and bemused, she told the teller, "That can't be. I just had a direct deposit to this account." After further research, the teller was able to determine that her mortgage company had taken three payments from her account in one month. Until the problem was resolved, her account would remain with a negative balance. While she debated her dilemma, she heard a still small voice whisper "Go to your mailbox. Your income tax check is there." She shook her head in disbelief and argued in her spirit with the voice. "That check can't be there. I filed late, and it has only been a week. There's no way that my check is in my mailbox."

She left the bank and headed to her mailbox; a small box grouped with those of others in her townhouse. Slowly, she put the key inside and saw one piece of mail inside. It was not this woman's habit of visiting her mailbox very often. Usually, the box was filled to overflowing with letters and ads. The woman closed her eyes and put the mail to her face. She prayed, then opened her eyes, and there was her federal income tax check in the amount of nearly $3,000. Rejoicing and giving God all the praise and glory, the woman immediately raced back to the bank to secure her account.

Sometimes, the still small voice of God can be heard in our spirit, but we ignore it. It can come as a miracle, as it did for this woman, or it can come as a warning. God does not yell at us; He whispers His messages. It is up to us to listen, pay attention, and immediately take the action that He instructs us to take.

"And after the earthquake a fire; but the LORD was not in the fire: and after the fire a still small voice." (I Kings 19:12).
"A form stood before my eyes, and I heard a hushed voice." (Job: 4:16)

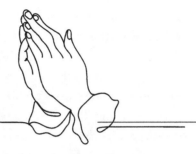

Prayer

Today, I will listen to hear your voice through the noise of this world. I will focus on the spiritual message you have for me. Help me to clear my mind and spirit, so that when You speak, I will know your voice and follow your guidance. In the holy name of Jesus Christ, Amen.

FRIDAY

A six-year-old child was taken to school for his first day in first grade. When his mother brought him inside, she and his new teacher explained that first grade was for big boys. It meant that he was growing up and he was expected to act like a young gentleman. Before the mother left, she told him she would be there to pick him up after school, just as she had when he was in kindergarten. The school day went on and the little boy was pleasant, but around noon, he picked up his book bag and headed for the door. "Where are you going?" his teacher asked. The child stared at her and in a matter-of-fact voice declared, "I'm going home. My mother is probably outside waiting for me." The teacher explained to the little boy that he was in first grade and school hours were different, longer than when he was in kindergarten. The child snatched his book bag off and threw it on the floor. He glared at the teacher and asked, "Who in the world signed me up for this crap?"

We all have that same childlike spirit when we believe we have stayed in the same place and the same situation far too long. We begin to question God and ask for a reprieve from financial woes, unruly children, a difficult marriage or relationship. Like this little boy, we wonder how we got into this situation and when we are going to get out of it. Scripture says, "Wait on the Lord be of good courage, and he shall strengthen thine heart: wait, I say, on the Lord." (Psalm 27:14).

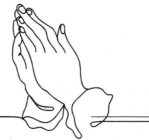

Dear Heavenly Father,

I know you are the timekeeper and "the author and finisher of my faith." (Hebrews 12:2). There are times when I feel abandoned and dismayed because of where I am and what is happening in my life. Give me the strength and the endurance to finish the race. Let me know that You are always there to pick me up. Your uplifting is always right on time. In the holy name of Jesus Christ I pray, Amen.

SATURDAY

A woman and her friend met at a neighborhood diner to discuss a few challenges the friend was facing. When they ordered their meal, the waitress began telling the woman about her boyfriend problems. This went on for about fifteen minutes, then finally, the two were able to order. While waiting for their meal, the friend began explaining her concern when someone in the booth behind them said excitedly, "Did somebody die? I died." The booth woman immediately began explaining how she died, came back to life, and was searching for a church that would allow her to give her testimony. The food arrived, but with every bite, someone in the restaurant began talking to the dining woman about some complication in their lives. Finally, the two decided to exit the diner. As they arose from their seats, a man yelled across the room asking the woman her advice on his issue. The friend stopped him and said "Huh uh…We're leaving now. Dr. Phil has left the building." The two laughed heartily as they left the diner.

Regardless of how strange or foolish the tale, everyone needs someone who is willing to listen. Although this seems to be an extreme case, the woman was accustomed to strangers soliciting her advice. She had long determined that it was her calling to be "the unpaid, unschooled psychologist with the aura of a priest." It seemed everyone was confessing to her. We all have a calling; something that is unique and different about our mission. God put it there to be used as a gift for the giver and the receiver. Jesus said, "Do not neglect to do good and to share what you have, for such sacrifices are pleasing to God."" (Hebrews 13:16).

Dear God,

Thank you for the gifts you have placed inside me. Thank you for the ability to use these gifts for your honor and your glory. I may not know or realize the special enlightenment that is in me. Please show me what it is and how to use it on earth for the sake of heaven. In Jesus holy and mighty name, I pray, Amen.

SUNDAY

Loretta's best friend had been stricken with a mysterious illness for more than a year. Since Loretta moved out of state, the two would talk frequently on the phone. One Friday night, Loretta received a call from her friend's mother stating that her friend had passed away that afternoon. Sandra was also a close friend to Loretta's best friend. In fact, the two had been childhood friends who attended school together and shared many confidences. She had also been diagnosed with a debilitating disease; however, she was still ambulatory and able to work. When Loretta received the call, she immediately called to make sure Sandra was alright. They engaged in mutual consolation.

At the funeral, Loretta and Sandra sat with the family, often reaching across other mourners to comfort one another. When the funeral procession reached the cemetery, the casket was opened to give everyone an opportunity for a final glimpse at their beloved. Loretta's mother walked beside her as she was leaving the site, sobbing uncontrollably. She suddenly remembered Sandra and went back to give her a hug. They embraced in a tight hold that lasted a minute or two, but when they broke their hold and started walking away, Sandra stumbled. Loretta and her mother grabbed her before she hit the ground, but it appeared that Sandra had fainted. After calling for medical assistance, it was too late. Sandra passed in the arms of Loretta and her mother, only twenty feet away from the coffin of her friend. The last touch of love, the final embrace, the concluding time of comfort and compassion left Loretta and her mother, then entered Sandra during her final moments on the earth.

When we hug someone or speak to someone, we are always transmitting our feelings. It is best not to toy with someone's emotions or play maniacal games with their hearts. We never know when a door is permanently closing, a voice is finally fading, or a gesture of good will is sending someone from here to eternity. God has a way of bringing the right people at the right time when we open our eyes to life and close our eyes in death.

"If one member suffers, all suffer together; if one member is honored, all rejoice together. " (I Corinthians 12:26)

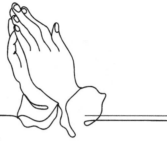

Dear Faithful Father,

Thank you for the people who bring joy and happiness to
my life. I pray that as I close my eyes for my final sleep,
you will allow a good-hearted, loving, and kind person to
celebrate what I was on the earth, and what I hope to be
in heaven. In the precious name of our Lord and Savior
Jesus Christ I pray, Amen.

Acknowledgements

I would like to thank my dear friend Andrew Jerrick for his inspiration. May he rest in eternal peace. My special thanks go to Dr. Judy Alsobrooks Meredith for being there through the good, the bad, the hurts, the humiliations, and the roughest years of my life, and teaching me how to laugh in the face of adversity.

I would also like to thank my family, James Flanders, Jr., Goldwyne Owusu, Gwendolyn Flanders Blackmon, Curtis Boyd, and especially my dear aunt Diane Porter for their lifelong support. I thank my dear friends Freda Barker and Dave Fiske for holding my hands through the bad times.

Bibliography

Aloysius, J. (n.d.). Farley. Retrieved from Merriam-Webster: http://www.merriam-webster.com/dictionary/farley

Brudney, K. D. (n.d.). Resurgence of Tuberculosis in New York City. American REview of REspiratory Disease, 144(No. 4), 745-749.

Fayer, S. H. (1990). Voices of Freedom. Blackside, Inc.

Garrow, D. (1999). Bearing the Cross. Quill Publishers.

Hague, S. (1997). "Niggers Ain't Gonna Run This Town". Department of History Loyola University, 1-19.

Hill, L. (1997). Deacons for Defense. Retrieved from Freedom Archives. com/Documents Finder: http://www.freedomarchives.org/Documents/Finder/Black%20Liberation%20Disk/Black%20Power!/SugahData/Dissertations/Hill.S.pdf

Kaufman, J. (1988). Broken Alliance: The Turbulent Times Between Blacks and Jews in America. Institute for Historical Review, 311.

Lowery, W. K. (2015, April 3). These are the racially charged e-mails that got 3 Ferguson police and court officials fired. Retrieved from The Washington Post: http://www.washingtonpost.com/news/post-nation/wp/2015/04/03/these-are-the-racist-e-mails-that-got-3-ferguson-police-and-court-officials-fired/

Meredith, J. (2012). A Mission from God.

Spurgeon, C. (1857, March 29). The Snare of rhe Fowler. New Park Street Pulpit. New York: Spurgeon Archives. Retrieved August 19, 2015, from http://www.spurgeon.org/sermons/0124.htm

staff, H. (2009). Nelson Mandela. (H. staff, Producer) Retrieved from History.com: http://www.history.com/topics/nelson-mandela

Swaine, J. L. (n.d.). Police brutality must be punished if we want real justice for Michael Brown. The Guardian. Retrieved from http://www.theguardian.com/us-news/2015/jun/01/black-americans-killed-by-police-analysis

Unknown. (n.d.). 1960: Civil Rights Movement Veterans. crmvet.org. Retrieved from http://www.crmvet.org/tim/timhis60.htm

Unknown. (2015, March 4). New York Times. Retrieved from Justice Department Report on Shooting of Michael Brown: http://www.nytimes.com/interactive/2015/03/04/us/doj-report-on-shooting-of-michael-brown.html?_r=0

Unknown. (2015, July 27). Tuberculosis: Causes, Symptoms, Treatments. Retrieved from Medical News Today: http://www.medicalnewstoday.com/articles/8856.php

CPSIA information can be obtained
at www.ICGtesting.com
Printed in the USA
BVHW081923020921
615904BV00002B/365